Green Smoothie Magic

More Than 132 Delicious, Adaptable Green Smoothie Recipes Using Easy To Find Ingredients

By Gabrielle Raiz

Thanks for purchasing this book, I hope you love it! Please review the book on Amazon – it will help me improve and make each version even better!

To get more **Green Smoothie Magic Tips & Tricks**, join my **Green Smoothie Magic Newsletter** (it's free!) – just use the link below:

http://www.GreenSmoothiesFromHeaven.com/tips

Gabrielle Raiz is the author of the best-selling book & DVD *"Hot Yoga MasterClass"* and the Principal of the Hot Yoga Teacher Training Program *"Hot Yoga Doctor Pro"*.

Visit my other sites!

http://www.HotYogaDoctor.com/

http://www.HotYogaMasterClass.com/

http://www.EasyHotYogaWeightloss.com/

http://www.HotYogaTeacher.com/

Disclaimer

Why it's advisable to give you a 'waiver' about the fact that eating well is good for you is frankly, beyond me. However, due to the way the world is these days, here it is:

This book is written with high intentions to share information about how to fit more raw fruit, vegetables, nuts, seeds and especially leafy green vegetables into your life. Who knows what kind of magic will happen in your life as a result of adapting your eating habits?

What you eat is up to you. You have to be careful to eat a full complement of nutritional foods to satisfy your nutritional needs. You probably won't get that out of one green smoothie. It comes from an approach that you take for your own good health.

This book makes no warranties, guarantees or promises to heal any illness nor does it promise that it will keep you young, make you look better, feel better, cure diseases, prevent diseases or stop the symptoms or signs of conditions or illnesses.

If you have questions about your own state of health it is always a good idea to consult people whom you trust, medicos and other health professionals. Perhaps you need to be reminded to 'consult your physician'.

This book is not a source of medical information and this book is not designed to render you any medical service. No book can be a substitute for your actions for direct, personal and or professional medical diagnosis and care. Understanding where you are at medically or nutritionally at this present moment is a great place to start, then make up your mind where you take it. It's up to you but you're not on your own.

There! It's done.

If you've ever wondered how to get a child to 'eat their greens', or scratched your head at how you could possibly eat enough 'raw food' to benefit from this health-boosting diet revolution …

… then learning to make delicious, healthy 'green' smoothies is a must.

I believe the theory is creatively brilliant – it's such a quick and easy way to benefit from the amazing nutritional punch packed into nature's green leafy vegetables.

Just blend them together and there you have an instantly healthy drink!

But beware. Not all green smoothie recipes are created equal – some require difficult to find ingredients while others depend on expensive 'superfoods'. Some combinations are simply horrible! (Believe me I know this from experience – I did the research!)

So while the idea is fantastic in theory, in practice you have to be careful that you end up with a palatable drink – preferably something yummy and delicious.

For example, some of the best raw greens are very strong in taste, so unless you want to feel as if you are drinking grass-clippings every day, then you'll want to know how to balance them in your recipes.

I recommend you start out with solid foundational recipes, using nature's easy-to-find and 'nutritionally dense' ingredients that you can obtain from your local markets or store.

Then, once you have a repertoire of successful recipes based on ingredients you'll ALWAYS have on hand, you'll be happy to adapt and experiment. If you want to add any of the more popular superfoods, (such as chia seeds or acai berries or spirulina for example) I'll show you how, though in this book, I've made sure you don't *need* them.

If you are brand new to green smoothies you'll probably want to develop your taste for them first as some combinations are definitely 'stronger tasting' than others. In this book you'll learn to make scrummy-yummy family-friendly smoothies that makes the start of the journey much easier.

EVERY recipe is tested – and contains substitutable ingredients.

I show you how to go about substituting and adapting ingredients … and even rescuing 'disasters'.

This drinkable 'raw-food-revolution' doesn't have to be the playground of the fringe-dweller. Green smoothies are well-within every person's taste, budget and lifestyle.

They ARE the ideal complete and 'fast' superfood!

Packed with practical information on how to make delicious green smoothies using easy-to-find ingredients, my hope with this book is you will soon have you wowing your family and friends with your extensive and delicious repertoire!

In it you will discover:

- More than 132 TESTED* delicious Green Smoothie recipes (including suggested variations!)

- Recommendations for adapting and substituting ingredients, depending on availability and taste

- How to make amazing green smoothies from regular ingredients - **Green Smoothie Magic** recipes do not require expensive specially marketed 'superfoods' (but there is a section on adding them when and if you want to!)

- How to rescue any smoothie that didn't quite turn out as expected!

- How to start getting great quality raw food nutrition into your lifestyle with no "taste shock"!

- The best ways to wash and store ingredients

- Blending and blender recommendations

* Yes, extensively tested on myself, my husband, daughter, family, friends and lots of my yoga students around the world!

Let's get started ...

Contents

Introduction **14**

If You Are New To Green Smoothies Start Here................................ 15

If You Don't Need The Information And Just Want The Recipes Start Here 16

Is It All Just Too Simple? 17

Super Smoothies Without The 'Superfoods' 18

Who Am I? 19

Are You Getting Enough? 21

The Lowest Common Denominator 22

How To Start Simply 22

Start Your Day The Way You Want To Continue 23

Meal Or Meal Replacement? 24

The Magic Of The Green Stuff **25**

Marketing Works - Unfortunately.. 25

Putting It All Back Together.. 26

Have You Heard Not To Do This? 27

Stop Doing SAD And Take Control 27

Alkali-Forming Foods 30

But I Can Eat A Salad! 30

Get More Out Of Your Greens 31

There's Protein In Them There Greens! 31

How Much Of My Smoothie Should Be Green? 35

Ingredient Quantities In This Book 36

Handfuls, Bunches Or Cups?.. 36

Which Vegetables Are Starchy? 37

Not All Green Smoothies Are Green **38**

Our Obsession With Food And The 'Best Way To Cook It'!.................... 38

Raw Food You Ask? 39

Tuning Into You 40

Don't Get Stuck With The Same Green 42

Knowing Your Greens – Substituting For Holistic Nutrition 42

Greens 44

Mix And Match 44

A List Of Mild Greens 44

Try Before You Take The Plunge 47

Can't Find Chickweed? Don't Know What It Is? 47

Lambsquarter? Pigweed? Purslane? Goosefoot? Fat-Hen? Yikes! 48

The Art Of Following Recipes: Two Types Of People 48

Choosing Your Greens: A Quick Primer 49

Storage And Use For Smoothies 49

TIP: Wash Your Greens As Soon As You Get Home! 49

Drying Your Greens 50

Storing Your Greens 50

Stems 50

Herbs In Water 51

Different Ingredients Add To Your Health And Help Weight Loss 52

How 'Green' Should My First Smoothies Be? 53

Green Smoothie Magic Basics 54

Should I Add Nut Milk Or Nuts? 54

Unlock The Living Magic 55

Using Nuts To Make Milk 57

Substitutions 57

It's Your Smoothie, So You Choose The Thickness 58

The Pragmatic Approach To Health, Nutrition And Everything! 60

Give It To Me Straight. What Are Superfoods? 61

Should You Eat Superfoods? 63

The Superfoods In *Green Smoothie Magic* 64

The Pragmatic Approach To Sprouts 71

Examples Of Sprouts And Microgreens 72

Freezing Fruit 74

How To Freeze Fruit For Smoothies 74

Green Smoothie 'Rescue' – What To Do If A Recipe Doesn't Work Out! 77

About Blenders And Blending 80

The Best Blenders For Smoothies 80

Choosing Your Blender 81

Various Blenders And Price Indications 82

Blending Techniques 83

About Drinking And Storing Your Smoothie 84

How Long Can You Keep Them? 84

How Long To Drink It (Gulp It Down?) 84

Drinking Your Smoothie Cold – Is Too Cold Bad? 84

The Best Way To Drink Your Smoothies 85

Time To Get Started! 85

Green Smoothie Magic 101: Instructions At A Glance For Blending Any Smoothie 86

How Much Will Each Recipe Make? 86

Reminder 1: What Greens To Use? 86

Reminder 2: Adding Water And Ice 86

Reminder 3: Nuts And Nut Milk 87

Reminder 4: Adding Sweeteners 88

Reminder 5: Adding In Superfoods 88

Reminder 6: Scoring smoothies 88

Reminder 7: Have Fun And Enjoy Your Smoothie Adventures 89

Recipe Index Cross-Referenced For Major Ingredient 89

Green Smoothie Magic Recipes 90

1. Classic Pine-Mint Smoothie... 90
2. Cinnamango Smoothie 91
3. Mangolicious Strawberry-Mint 91
4. Bananaberry Cream 92
5. Mango Delight 92
6. Vanilla Chai Smoothie 93
7. Choc-Chai Smoothie 94
8. Banana-Choc-Chai Smoothie 95
9. Banana Raspberry Yum 96
10. Berrylicious.. 97
11. Pineapple Broccoli Sensation 97
12. Pineapple Dilly Dally 98
13. Herbal Ginger Beet 99
14. Saladicious.. 100
15. Salad Sunset 101
16. Blue Bat 102
17. Blueberry Pineapple Smoothie... 103
18. Berry Packed Smoothie 103
19. What A Lovely Pear 104
20. Tangy Tex Mex 105
21. Dance To The Beet 105
22. Mango Spice 106
23. Choc-Mango Spice... 107
24. Blue Eyes Smoothie 108
25. Vanilla Pudding Smoothie 109
26. Carob Vanilla Spice Pudding Smoothie 110
27. Mint Vanilla Pudding Smoothie 111
28. Kiwi Vanilla Smoothie.. 112
29. Freshly Minted 113
30. Iron Maiden Smoothie 114

31.   Mint Magic 114

32.   Stevie's Punch 115

33.   Kiwi Dill Elixir 116

34.   Strawberry Kiwi Sunshine 116

35.   Minted Pear Smoothie 116

36.   Lime Ginger Dill Smoothie 117

37.   Poppy Celebration Smoothie 118

38.   Fennel Refresher 119

39.   Apricana Smoothie 120

40.   On Blueberry Dill 121

41.   Raspberry Serenade 121

42.   Mango Carob Dessert Smoothie 122

43.   Mango Crème Carabel 123

44.   Minted Crème Carabel 124

45.   Bananazilla Smoothie 125

46.   Date With An Orange 126

47.   Orange Cinnamon Paradiso 126

48.   The B.O.S.S. 127

49.   Tomango Fandango 127

50.   Pacific Paradise 128

51.   Summer Lite 128

52.   Savory Spice 129

53.   Berry Cress 129

54.   Kiwi Krave 130

55.   Beet This! 130

56.   Heavenly Rocket 131

57.   Mint Skyrocket 132

58.   Green Rocket Booster 132

59.   Tropical Vertigo 133

60.   Raspberry Banana Sunshine 134

61.   Pineapple Pick-Me-Up 135

62. Chocolate Charm 135

63. Strawberry Mint Memento 136

64. Carob-Mint Caress 137

65. Red Rocket Smoothie 138

66. Tropical Red Rocket 139

67. CeleryBration 140

68. Pineapple Earth-Shaker 140

69. Pineapple Pesto 141

70. Aromango 141

71. Bright Limey 142

72. Classic Pear Smoothie 143

73. Silky Pear 143

74. Mon Pear 144

75. The Green Smile 144

76. Pine Zinger 144

77. Strawbanana Crush 145

78. Salsa Me Smooth 146

79. Quick And Easy Mint Smoothie 147

80. Quick And Easy Mint Smoothie Mark 2 147

81. Berry Appealing 148

82. Classic Banana 149

83. Classic Mango 150

84. Coco-De-Menthe 150

85. Classic Strawberry 151

86. Rocket Mango Tango 151

87. Gone Troppo 152

88. Majestic Mango Mint 153

89. Velvet Mango Mint 153

90. Apple Tang 153

91. Coco-Nana 154

92. Kiwi Parsley Punch 155

93. Italian Summer 155

94. Not Just Peachy 156

95. Cinnamon Celery Sensation 156

96. English Pears 157

97. Cream Apple-Mint 158

98. Loves Me Like A Brocc 158

99. Perfectly Peared 159

100. StrawPear-Ease 159

101. Tropical Surprise 160

102. Herbed Cleanser 160

103. Sweet Sunrise 161

104. Dappled Greens 161

105. Strawberry Dills Forever 162

106. Minted Blue 163

107. Raspberry Crush 164

108. Pear-ly There 165

109. Basil Beauty 165

110. Raspberry Dream 166

111. Bali Sunrise 166

112. Minty Miracle 167

113. Dessert Pear 168

114. Refreshingly Herbal Pear 169

115. Sweet Dill Surprise 169

116. Savory Papaya 170

117. Sweet Savory Papaya 170

118. Pakito Kicker 171

119. Pakito Kiss 171

120. Amazing Grape 172

121. Lemon Spinner 172

122. Lemony Sippet 173

123. Lemon Digestive 174

124.   Queen Of Cress 175

125.   Papaya Cream Pudding 176

126.   Oatmeal Breakfast Smoothie 177

127.   Ki-Wheat Wonder 178

128.   Ki-Wheat Minty Marvel 178

129.   BlueGrass 179

130.   Creamy Green Supreme 179

131.   Summer Meadows 180

132.   Citrus Cocktail 180

Recipe Index Cross-Referenced For Major Ingredient 182

Apple/Pear 183

Avocado 184

Mango/Papaya 186

Banana 188

Pineapple 188

Berries 190

Citrus (Orange, Lemon, Lime) 191

Dried Fruit and Dates 192

Unconventional Smoothie Vegetables! 194

Nuts, Seeds or Nut/Seed Milk 195

Green Smoothie Magic

Tired of smoothie books with too much 'theory and so-called science' and a handful of recipes – when what you really want are tons of recipes and practical tips?

Well, I will certainly give you plenty of practical information to help you make successful, delicious smoothies, generously balanced by over 132 green smoothie recipes (and variations).

I'll also give you some background information to serve you a big dose of motivation – "why" you should be doing this in the first place – just to make sure you know the reason why we do certain things in the wonderful world of green smoothies!

I have written this book so that each section pretty much stands alone in the context of green smoothies, so that you can dip into it at any point and still make sense of the subject. Because of this, you will find from time to time that there is a small amount of repetition. I trust that this will help you and that you can put up with that!

I want to honor everyone who will read this book. The green smoothie 'newbies' who are new to the smoothie, healthy food, or even raw and vegan bandwagons, as well as those who are simply expanding their green smoothie recipe collections.

Importantly too, my aim is to bust some myths that you may have heard or read about, and I want to let you in on a very practical approach to health, green smoothies and more.

As a yoga teacher I like to tell people that why something happens is not nearly as important as the fact that it DOES.

So you don't need to know the theory behind green smoothies to experience their magic. You simply have to start. If you're a first timer, then feel free to jump in by finding a few smoothie recipes that tickle your fancy and then just dip into the smoothie information sections whenever you feel like learning more.

Introduction

Green smoothies are well ... green! Maybe not green in color, although many of them are, but they are green in contents. They may be fruit blended with some of nature's other magical ingredients. Some are light and fresh and tangy. Others are smooth, luxuriant, sweet and creamy. Others have a citrus note, others taste more herb-laden.

Whatever your goals, whether it's your quest for vibrant health, weight loss or shape management, incorporating green smoothies will be the revelation you have been looking for! Welcome to *Green Smoothie Magic*.

There is no greater gift than the gift of great health.

Taking this positive step is the way to give back to yourself and in a way where you can feel the results in your body and the clarity in your mind. Bold claims eh? To the *Green Smoothie Magic* uninitiated these may seem like lofty assertions! So rather than taking my word for it, you've taken the plunge, you've bought this book (and I humbly thank you) so now it's time to get started.

With the modern age of processed foods there's a move away from home prepared foods in favor of pre-packaged food and less of an emphasis on fresh produce. With so many enticements to move away from the kinds of foods we should be eating one really has to be careful not to stray too far from the (garden?) path.

When you take control and start pumping in the good nutrients that processed stuff becomes far less attractive. You're even likely to find your cravings will morph, your shopping habits right along with them.

While I don't believe in making generalized health claims, I do know for a fact that most people don't eat enough of 'the good stuff'. Everyone has their tastes! Most of these tastes have been shaped by years of habits. What you eat was largely what your family ate and what their families ate before them.

I am positive that there are not many people who would dare to dispute that, on the whole, our diets are sadly lacking. We all KNOW that when it comes to the essentials, you really cannot go past fresh, raw fruit and vegetables.

While fruits are seen as the easy way to get some of your important foods in, it does seem the green leafy stuff and many vegetables in general continue to get a bad rap. This is where *Green Smoothie Magic* comes in.

There are many theories and explanations for so many benefits of particular 'diets'. This book is not intended to explore these in depth.

Whether you're vegetarian, vegan or an omnivore who loves their meat, this book is about taking control of your health. It's about taking a practical approach to finding balance. The magic of green smoothies is that you can reclaim that true satisfaction of *really* eating well.

This may even be satisfaction that you will discover for the very first time. With that you're very likely to find that your habits transform into ways that will support you to find strength and health.

If You Are New To Green Smoothies Start Here

Thank you for buying this book! If you're new to making or drinking green smoothies then it's important to take the plunge and make and drink these amazing concoctions. It's far less important to read all the information. That could sound odd coming from the author, but to be clear, it's acting on the impulse that got you here that is the key to making a difference in your life.

If you just want to jump right in without reading the entire introduction (which is quite detailed) then I highly recommend you start your journey by reading the section entitled ***Green Smoothie Magic 101: Instructions At A Glance For Blending Any Smoothie.***

The instructions that you will find come as a list of 7 reminders. They were all extracted from expanded information in the previous sections so you can go and research more depth in any subject.

Whatever you need clarification on will become evident to you and you can select different sections appropriate to your needs directly from the contents.

As I mentioned previously, this book is designed for you to 'dip in' and get what you need. That means you will find that each section can be read on its own without too much cross-referencing. In order to do that, there is a small amount of repetition in the book to facilitate the 'at-a-glance' nature of the book.

Other chapters that are worth looking at before you start (as a beginner)

Take a look at the topics covered in the table of contents. I recommend getting some information about using greens. In the 'Greens' section you will find a heading that will take you to a very long list of the different mild green leafy vegetables and a shorter list of strong greens. Using the table of contents you will be able to instantly navigate to both these lists. If nothing else it will give you confidence and give you a road map to be able to create delicious smoothies with literally dozens of greens you may not have ever considered using before.

You may find that understanding why to vary the greens you use will empower you to greater health. Find such a chapter by navigating from the contents to **Don't Get Stuck With The Same Green.**

You do not need to read all the theory to make great green smoothies. Don't feel pressured to read from cover to cover just because you bought the book. Do however, dip in and find some recipes to get the ball rolling.

If You Don't Need The Information And Just Want The Recipes Start Here

I know there will be many people who purchase this book (thank you too!) who have been making green smoothies for ages. Maybe you do not want to wade through more information but just want to go to the recipes.

So, it's handy to know that just before the 132 recipes there is a short section called **Green Smoothie Magic 101: Instructions At A Glance For Blending Any Smoothie.** These few pages will help you understand the way I have presented all the recipes in this book. These come as a list of 7 reminders. All those reminders are expanded upon in previous sections so you can go and research more depth in any subject.

I've also included a short note after the reminders explaining the "**Recipe Index Cross-Referenced For Major Ingredient**" - which is a section at the BACK of the book allowing you to see lists of recipes sorted by their major ingredient. Just click on any recipe title and you'll be taken straight to it. I've put this at the back of the book because I believe you will get more enjoyment from the book initially by browsing the information and the recipes - but as you progress, you may have some ingredients on hand and be wondering "now which recipe do I fancy today?". In which case, this is the section for you!

My approach to using nuts and superfoods may be different to what you have been used to. So please decide after reading your 7 reminders whether you want to selectively read other portions of this book! Have fun in your smoothie-licious adventures.

Is It All Just Too Simple?

It does seem that way. Here we are in the modern age of astonishing medical breakthroughs, pharmaceutical concoctions that are claimed to cure just about every ill known to mankind. And then come the food fundamentalists (haha) who say, 'hold on a second, take a look at how you eat in the first place'.

Far be it for me to make medical claims about drinking green smoothies. In fact, I won't. I could write a book hundreds of pages long citing anecdotal evidence where thousands upon thousands of people just like you and me have created, regained or sustained vibrant health simply by changing the food that they eat.

Thousands more will tell you that they have lost weight, regained their former trim figures and toned any excess fat by eating well.

But is it too good to be true? Maybe.

It's not just about finding the perfect potion. It's about embracing an approach that is well-aligned with the essence of our human being-ness.

We weren't created to eat the latest greatest pre-packed highly-processed enticingly marketed pasta sauce, yoghurt, soda or potato chip. So it's really no surprise to me that ANYONE can have health and wellbeing at their fingertips when they eat more fruit and vegetables and cook way less than they did before.

I don't call that detoxing. That's a concept that has become a billion dollar industry. Although – and for this we can be grateful – it is getting people to think about what they should and shouldn't eat. However, in my not so humble opinion, it is gearing people towards believing that they need expensive products. Not so!

Do people lose weight or feel better on a detox? Well yes, they do! And it probably has little to do with those special proprietary products.

Ever noticed that for detox regimes those taking part usually drink juice, have smoothies, or water with lemon juice, cayenne and maple syrup. For many programs that's ALL you have for days or weeks at a time. I mean, who wouldn't lose some pounds or feel cleansed after that?

So it's really about taking control. How you got here to read this book is frankly not as important as where you go from here. Whether you call taking control of your health a 'detox', a 'diet' or a 'sensible plan' it really doesn't matter. What matters is that the evidence IS there:

If you eat MORE raw vegetables and fruit, if you eat PLENTY of green leafy vegetables then your health is likely to improve. It could be better than it ever has been before.

Super Smoothies Without The 'Superfoods'

You are hearing more and more about them, but what IS a 'superfood'? To me there are 'superfoods' and superfoods. In a nutshell there are certain foods that are marketed with claims that they are 'the' answer to creating glowing health that you may not get with other foods.

So in this section I'm going to take a pragmatic approach to superfoods.

It is my belief that science has only really scratched the surface when it comes to uncovering and understanding the nutrition that wholefoods bring to you and me. Scientists can tell us that there are certain elements to a piece of broccoli but they don't understand the magic of the synergy of it as a wholefood.

Just because you know that something (imagine here a box of breakfast cereal) has certain antioxidants, has specific amounts of certain fats, amino acids and so on and so forth, doesn't mean you can quantify good health or the effect of that food on the body.

If you happen to be unwell then sometimes science – through tools such as blood analyses – may be able to tell you where you may need a boost in your nutrition. If you need iron then (beyond getting your initial and perhaps acute needs met by a supplement) it is far better for you to find out what wholefoods have iron in them than taking a supplement.

Far better to know that overall you're eating foods that have the building blocks you need and then let nature provide the invisible keys to get on with the job of creating or sustaining some level of health.

By the way, while I do take some vitamins and other nutrients (which are themselves made of wholefoods and not chemical derivatives) I don't believe that one should substitute a pill for eating well. Getting a good balance of nutrients is your primary goal.

What you'll gain from using the principles and recipes in this book is that when you make and consume a variety of greens and a variety of green smoothies, you will create a great balance. There are certain so-called 'superfoods' that will help you boost certain aspects of nutrition.

Within these pages you'll find recipes that use wholefoods and superfoods. Hmmm. What IS a superfood? That definitely depends on your definition. To me a superfood is generally wholefood that is thoughtfully cultivated without pesticides and ideally organic. These foods have good solid nutritional profiles. You can refer to superfoods as 'nutritionally dense'.

To the public at large however, and because of the wonders of internet marketing, a 'superfood' is generally an expensive product (usually more expensive when it's described by the word 'superfood') that often comes from an exotic sounding destination. The jury is out on whether these 'superfoods' contain EXTRA benefit to the ones we find in the fresh food section of the (super)market.

It's absolutely fine to put these foods into your smoothies (I'll give you guidelines for doing this and a list, should this be something you want to pursue.) I don't want to marginalize anyone because of their beliefs or even their ability to afford some of these expensive products.

So, I will make some recommendations as to where and how to use certain 'superfoods' but you will rarely find them essential to any of the recipes. I live by the credo that good health and a great green smoothie recipe is within the reach of everyone.

Who Am I?

Hahaha. Isn't that a question we all have to ask ourselves. Some people think it's important to know who's writing this tome. So here goes …

After high school (I went to the Conservatorium of Music) I graduated as a dentist (naturally). It all seems so long ago. I practiced dentistry for many years and decided that despite loving what I did, it was time to branch out and explore life on different terms and in different ways.

Since high school (which I finished over 30 years ago – you do the math) I have been involved in the health industry. From dentist to being a manager in a pharmaceutical company to opening Australia's very first healthy fast food store. We were nationally endorsed by the Heart Foundation and served healthy food (nothing deep fried, natural flavors, fresh innovative fast food) that also happened to be vegetarian. Yup, so delicious that even the local butcher chose to eat there.

Fast forward a little more and my fascination for holistic health and great food keeps evolving.

I have moved more and more into incorporating raw foods into my diet. I also got married and became a Bikram yoga teacher . I completed Bikram's course in LA and have become a world renowned 'hot-yoga-technical-and-all-things-yoga expert', answering questions, solving people's yoga problems the world over and spending a lot of time writing. I have written a successful book on the subject of yoga too! (If you're curious to find out more, there's a link in the front of the book.)

Sometime after becoming a yoga teacher I gave birth to our adorable daughter. At the time of writing this book she's 9 and a half.

I have now come full circle with this book. I have combined my love of how the body works, nutrition and health (and writing about them!) into one. I have a very pragmatic approach to food, to the body, to hot yoga and yoga. I love cooking (regular style but admittedly my focus has evolved increasingly to include more raw food). I love un-cooking (raw food preparation) and can do both well.

I really enjoy putting food together into satisfying meals. I enjoy cooking fusion meals with raw and a smaller cooked component. For me, the healthier the meal, the more satisfying. Above all I want TASTE to reign supreme.

I must admit that I do occasionally indulge in things that others might consider (but I don't like to call) 'treats' and even sometimes – dare I say – eat some that verge on the unhealthy.

I live a healthy and balanced life and encourage you to find ways to do the same with balance and never, ever feeling any food-guilt. I am personally a vegetarian but I am not a veg-evangelist. I want you to follow your intuition and find your own way nutritionally.

You will find that making the move towards a rich plant-based way of life (no matter what food styles you prefer, meat or no meat) and using green smoothies as a staple will create a great and even unsurpassed feeling of wellbeing.

Creating this book has been a joy because I have been able to combine flavors together in ways I have never done before.

It's inevitable that some combinations are sooo good you'll see them recreated in other places. The difference in **Green Smoothie Magic** is that I'll show you how to adapt and evolve your OWN yummy versions or variations. Just wait until you start combining some of these more 'unexpected' combinations.

My wish is that you find tremendous satisfaction with each and every **Green Smoothie Magic** recipe in this book. It would be crazy for me to promise you that you will love every single smoothie. Maybe you are not partial to bananas or maybe you don't like pineapple. Never fear, I will have a list of substitutions for you. Funnily enough, both Robert and I never liked bananas! But for some reason we can both enjoy green smoothies with them in. Go figure!

So, I have tested all these recipes and I really like them (to different degrees too!). I have sought feedback and scores from many other people too! I like them all but I cannot like them all equally. It just depends. I prefer different smoothies at different times. What I like today may be something I have no desire for, for the next 2 weeks.

Allow yourself to experience the changes of your own food and taste preferences. Some smoothies will be lighter and more refreshing. Others will be more like an indulgent dessert or pudding that you spoon out and enjoy one small mouthful at a time. Some are sweet, some have just a hint of sweetness, some savory, some spicy, some hot and spicy. Some are more sour. Some with lots of herbs.

How delighted you are with the feeling of health and wellbeing that YOU create in yourself and perhaps in your family, will determine the choices you make around how many smoothies you do have per day.

Perhaps like me you'll start snacking on smoothies as a mini-meal. After all you know that eating a lesser amount more often is another key to vibrant health and longevity.

Are You Getting Enough?

So let me ask you: Are you missing out on the most incredible power-packed nutrition?

It can be so hard to eat enough of the very thing that nutritional science (and yes YOUR BODY) says you need in large amounts. That's right, green leafy vegetables! You see, most people find it very hard to fit in an amount that will actually create vibrant health.

Most people eat what they eat (and that is either going to be centered around animal flesh and or cooked grains and legumes) with a small green salad on the side. When what you should be doing is having raw salad (or the prepared ingredients of that raw salad) as the main part of how you sustain and nourish yourself.

So THAT'S what green smoothies are ALL about. You know, even though my family has been vegetarian for 18 years there have been times – I can assure you – where the salads and the raw life-giving stuff have, well ... um, taken a back seat and sometimes have been missing.

My daughter, who at the time of writing is less than 10, loves being vegetarian but trying to cram the right amount of green leafies into her is frankly a daunting task. That is UNTIL GREEN SMOOTHIES. I have been making these for a couple of years. Mind you, I had to start with smoothies that didn't have that green color. That's easy, make them berry based!

The great news is, that now she wants to make her own. She willingly throws in handfuls of greens and then enjoys her creations. So, sometimes in the recipes you'll see what score my 9 year old has given a particular smoothie. Perhaps you'll find this will be a wonderfully useful barometer for your own family's and friends' experiences.

The Lowest Common Denominator

Green smoothies are your key to health no matter what your diet choices are. You can use this incredible way to supplement no matter what way you eat. You need vegetables, you need fruit and you DEFINITELY need greens. It's really a no-brainer that green leafy vegetables are the most basic source of health on this planet.

Put it this way, if you want to search for something healthy in the supermarket you're often going to find the color green generously applied to the packaging (whether the product is healthy or not). Let's move on to how to actually incorporate these little wonders into your life.

How To Start Simply

So you've made the decision. Here's how to start the ball rolling. **Have one green smoothie per day**. There are different ways to do this.

Start Your Day The Way You Want To Continue

The best way to start your day is with your best foot forward, if you know what I mean. ;) So, if you're a breakfast person, substitute your cereal, toast, coffee, oatmeal or whatever with a nutritious power-packed green smoothie. If your main goal is to lose weight then green smoothies in the morning will give you the energy for the first part of the day and will get you started on the right foot.

From there you'll find it much easier to make better food choice decisions as you move forward. It could be that when you start the day with a green smoothie that you feel just so darn good that you (in most cases) just NATURALLY gravitate towards more good food. It's so much easier to continue eating well when you've started your day well.

When you eat well, it is suggested that your body is finally getting enough nutrients of the RIGHT kind. This means that you don't need to overeat, or unconsciously search for the things your body needs by taking in the wrong types of food (and by over-eating).

My friend Kay used to need to get her 'energy up' with a strong coffee as the very first thing she would have. Imagine when I asked her to switch over to a green smoothie. Well, she now swears that this is THE power kick that she needs and practically never drinks coffee anymore, ever.

Meal Or Meal Replacement?

Use it as a meal or as your first course (before) a meal. Green smoothies can be quite filling and you'll feel empowered while feeling satisfied yet somehow very light. Work your way up from there. Maybe you'll start taking green smoothies as snacks too (which would in all intents and purposes make your meals smaller). It's onward and upward.

Green Smoothie Weight Loss And Cleansing

It's not my intention to tell you to replace all your meals with green smoothies. You CAN of course for a set and pre-determined time. There are times where, if you're on a regime of cleansing foods, perhaps for weight loss, where you could consider some or all your meals for a limited period of time to be replaced by smoothies.

In any case, you will notice, that you'll be more interested in fresher, cleaner foods. So don't be surprised that, if instead of your 'same-old same-old' Monday night dinner (or habitual food choices you make anytime), you decide you want a huge salad with a little something else on the side. Yes, the scales will be tipped in your good health's favor – naturally.

The Magic Of The Green Stuff

I recommend you strive for balance. For as long as I can remember I have been aiming to put lots of different colors on the plate of my meals and that of my family. It helps to ensure that we all receive as full a spectrum of ingredients and micro-nutrients as is possible.

The wonderful thing about modern science is that it can break everything down into little component parts, which is great when it comes to your quest for understanding ... but there is a hidden catch that has influenced our thinking when it comes to nutrition.

Marketing Works - Unfortunately

Unfortunately where modern science lets us down in MANY cases, especially when it comes to new marketing trends, is to ignore the synergy of ingredients that occur in wholefoods. Food manufacturers are oh so busy showing us the fat, carbohydrate, protein and antioxidant components of their new fandangled package of highly processed food.

Meanwhile the miracles of wholefood alchemy are sitting on the shelves and in the fields, in the markets and in our gardens.

And guess what? NONE of those little beauties have a label on them.

Your mind becomes convinced with the 'legitimacy' of the typed ingredients and breakdown of all those wonderful (and possibly chemically derived) nutrients. Then your mind gets busy 'making the case' to support you buying the packaged stuff instead of the fresh, unprocessed and frankly comparatively unsexy or unenticing natural unprocessed fare.

Science is great for 'deconstructing things'. What YOU need to do is to take that information and then assess and integrate things that are WHOLE now that you have that greater understanding.

On the one hand it's important for you to know that your greens are:

- alkaline (a major focus of raw foods and eating the green stuff!)

- full of protein and amino acid building blocks!

- low in carbs (carbohydrates)

- high in fiber

- high in vitamins and minerals

- high in those colors such as chlorophyll and carotenoids giving them their green and yellow, orange and red pigments

- rich in essential fatty acids essential for energy production (includes your omega 3 and 6 fatty acids)

- and high in those antioxidants we're so keen on including ... because marketing giants use modern nutritionism and science to promote bits of their food.**

And on the other hand it's important to know that the synergy of eating whole fresh foods cannot be equaled by any *processed* food that claims to have all the above ingredients.

Putting It All Back Together

There is no science that explains the magic of wholefoods and the way that even undiscovered or un-researched elements of food nutrients work together to create, maintain or sustain your body in health.

In other words, breaking foods down to understand what's in them is only part of the picture. The real miracles are in the consuming of the whole unchanged food itself. You have to piece the puzzle back together.

** I discovered the truth about modern nutritionism in Michael Pollan's book, "*In Defense Of Food*". It's a very interesting read, I highly recommend you buy your own copy – or just borrow it from your library!

Have You Heard Not To Do This?

I actually do not count calories. I tried that many years ago when I was overweight. For most people it simply means that you are focusing on the wrong thing. Also, to count calories presumes that every *body* had the same ability to burn energy in the same way from the same food sources or doing the same activities.

This is simply not true. Your rate of metabolism is surely different to mine. The efficiency of your body is going to depend on the way you've treated it up until now, not just what you choose to feed it from now.

I have learned that it is not the calories that matters, it is far more important to eat fresh, lots of raw, well-chosen produce, mostly fruit and vegetables, with sources of the nutrients that every human being needs. A vegan is going to have to make different choices to an omnivore.

Remember that *bioavailability* of the nutrients you ingest is what you're actually looking for. In other words, how much of the good stuff is getting IN to your system to be used to your benefit. That equation will change with your health, your state of stress, your activity levels and wellbeing.

Nutritional tables are only a guide or line in the sand. They are not something you can live by. After all they belong to the world of modern nutritionism which is driven by big business. As I implied just above, the nutritional table on a green smoothie may be similar to a boxed processed food. Does this make them equal? Does this make the nutrients as good out of the box? I think not.

So I have deliberately left out nutritional tables. You have to take responsibility. Eat varied greens, a variety of nuts, seeds, good fats and oils and so on, with a wide variety of colors and nutrients. Make what you do natural and driven by your experience, knowledge and intuition.

You can't live by the numbers on a table and it's impossible to calculate the quantities across your meals. So take the sensible route.

You may be wise to get your blood tested and see where you may need to boost some levels. You can do that short term with supplements but now that you're a green smoothie drinker you will be able to add in more of the right 'stuff' into your smoothies because you know that nutrients taken from good sources IN your food makes them more bioavailable.

Stop Doing SAD And Take Control

S.A.D. is an acronym referring to the **S**tandard **A**merican **D**iet. It's a great pity that the rest of the world has trends that are similar. In fact with the proliferation of big multinational companies many developing nations are now developing the same disease states and conditions as we have already in the western world, en masse.

They call this an obesity epidemic and other crises to take the focus away from the root cause. It all starts with how we choose to nourish ourselves. What you feed you and your family REALLY MATTERS.

Unfortunately many processed unhealthy fat and sugar-laden foods are seductively inexpensive and become delicious to the eater. Oh, and rather amazingly, many of these seductive and nutritionally void foods are very, very cheap.

Two wonderful expressions come to mind:

- **Garbage in, garbage out**

- **You are what you eat.**

Just about every important disease state and condition that inflicts the human race finds its roots in poor nutrition. Even the FDA has published this finding on more than one occasion. Here is one quote from their website: *"There is more evidence than ever that dietary choices have major impacts on population health."*

http://www.fda.gov/Food/LabelingNutrition/LabelClaims/QualifiedHealthClaims/QualifiedHealthClaimsPetitions/ucm096010.htm

You not only need to feed yourself well, there are essential activity (exercise) and sun exposure levels. This would be a very long handbook indeed if we started to go down that path.

If you eat animal products then I won't say it's the wrong thing to do. However I do believe that *minimizing* the amount of flesh and dairy products will greatly benefit you.

I strongly believe that incorporating at least 60% raw fruit and vegetables into your diet is essential for you to have the building blocks for vibrant health. Ideally I would recommend upwards of 80% raw food. (But that's just me!) Still working with or towards those figures, still allows you to have those taste-cravings satisfied. I totally acknowledge that your choice is free.

This book is based on vegan recipes. Often you will have the choice to add in a nut or seed milk. Sometimes that will be as simple as adding a handful of nuts to your smoothie for an initial blend with water before you add the other ingredients.

If you have a really good blender you will be able to blend all ingredients once and be done with it. You'll learn more about blenders and blending later in the book.

You'll create creamy and smooth tasting smoothies in this way. You'll also be adding some other sources of fats, vitamins and minerals that will round out your own nutrition profile.

If you love dairy and if you believe it's essential for your health then you could consider adding in dairy milk instead of water, nut or seed milks. However I would strongly urge you to research the calcium leaching properties of all animal products.

While it is commonly promoted by certain groups that drinking dairy milk will add calcium to your body, the evidence seems to indicate the exact opposite. These are from reputable clinical studies. So please, do your homework first. Play it safe and avoid cow's milk products in your smoothies.

Here is a website for you to look at. This first one is not at all an attractive looking site: www.notmilk.com. I am not at all affiliated with this website nor do I receive any benefit by you going there. I simply add it because it has many clinical papers referenced and could be a good place for you to start.

If you decide to go there take a look at the index on the left side and maybe start with something like osteoporosis (http://www.notmilk.com/o.html) or heart disease (http://www.notmilk.com/h.html).

Each page will have many references to clinical studies and papers by scientists. So it's really worth a look. There are plenty of other websites. Whether or not any website has 100% trustworthy information I cannot say. They can be quite strongly worded and have information that you could be surprised and shocked by.

Do your own research. Try 'milk myths' as a search term. This is definitely an important subject. If nothing else doing this research will help you question what you're being told by readily available regurgitated (pardon the cow pun) information.

Fortify Your Body

Your food has the most incredible ability to fortify your body against many, many conditions. If you've ever met anyone with a heart condition such as high cholesterol or high blood pressure or diabetes then you'd probably be aware that one thing that they must take control of is their diet.

If you are diabetic then I encourage you to take a nutritional approach and look at incorporating raw food as your main focus. Please do your research. There is wonderful evidence out there that people with heart conditions, thyroid conditions, diabetes, even multiple sclerosis have had miraculous recoveries, reversals and improvements of different levels by eating more raw food (and some 'go completely raw').

I strongly recommend you check out "Simply Raw: Reversing Diabetes in 30 Days"

While my book is not about the raw food phenomenon, (which incidentally I put great faith in as well as a move away from the modern day profit-based pharma-culture) just know that **Green Smoothie Magic** has over 132 recipes that will arm you with tools for creating or regaining your birth right: Vibrant life-giving health.

Alkali-Forming Foods

It's not just me that says this. The more raw food and the more greens the better off you are. One of the reasons is that you create a more alkaline environment in your body. In 1931 Dr Warburg won the Nobel Prize for demonstrating that cancer and disease live in acidic environments (that can also be devoid of oxygen).

His research kicked off a wealth of research and results. Much of this points to the fact that disease states thrive in acidic conditions. Further it appears that one should eat foods that will create a more alkaline environment. Good food (mostly organic and raw) with plenty of green leafy vegetables, a complement of fruit, good quality sea salt and some exercise are keys to your health.

But I Can Eat A Salad!

You may say that you already eat well. If you've purchased this book (and I thank you for that!) then you either have a great or growing awareness around what is good nutrition.

The amazing thing that green smoothies do is to power-pack enormous amounts of the nutrients and goodness of those incredible greens into an easy to drink and easy to digest format.

I LOVE salad. At dinner times we have somewhere between 1 and 5 different raw salads. The easiest way to make the salad the main focus of your eating life is to make great ones.

Smoothies allow you to have these highly nutritious greens in your 'diet' in far greater quantities than most people would eat at one sitting. Of course, if you would generally eat that amount at one sitting then that's still wonderful. Making green leafy vegetables palatable for just about anyone is where smoothies really come into their own.

Let me put it this way: It is a veritable chore convincing my daughter to eat one tiny broccoli floret. Now I can give her a smoothie that has 2 handfuls of broccoli and she enjoys it. Yippee.

It's a win-win situation. She gets the benefits of a more balanced 'diet' with a truly magnificently nutritious vegetable and the whole family feels great about that.

Get More Out Of Your Greens

You have a choice. You can juice your fruit and vegetables and you can blend them. There are reasons to do both. I really love the feeling of a good juice. I often create a beet, carrot, ginger, kale juice with a squeeze of lemon. It's refreshing and delicious.

You get a ton of nutrients immediately available with juicing. However, what juices miss out on providing is a good amount of soluble and insoluble dietary fiber. Fiber is one of the keys to a well-functioning digestive and excretion system.

There is no juicing in this book. When I am making a smoothie, I really don't want to clean 2 machines. I love juicing but I don't want to clean the juicer because a recipe calls for ½ a cup of carrot juice.

When you blend your fruit and vegetables (such as when you create your smoothie magic) you want to have the nutrients, the fiber and all the goodness you can extract so it's available pronto. Breaking down the cell walls in your greens by blending is the key to extracting the most you can. When the cell walls are pulverized the nutrients are more readily available to your body.

When it comes to greens I don't think there's a more *accessible* nutritionally packed easily ingestible food on the entire planet.

There's Protein In Them There Greens!

Just about every vegetarian or vegan I know has been asked at one time or another a very curious (and sometimes silly and infuriating) question: *"Where do you get your protein?"*

A not so silly answer is to point people in a couple of directions. One is to let them know that at a human's most important growth period, as babies, that breast milk can solely sustain a child for months and months and it only has 1.1% protein, and only 6% of the calories from this milk are provided by that protein.

The other great fact is that the largest animals on the planet (apart from whales) including elephants, hippos, rhinos, gorillas and long lean strong giraffes are all vegetarian or herbivores. That's an impressive (and incomplete) list.

Protein is important for growth and if you're a child they're more important than for an adult. They are important for repair too. Be careful not to include too much protein. Those diets that are low carbs and high protein overwhelm the system in many ways, especially the kidneys.

Go for balance in your food choices. You don't need to do anything fancy. Eat a variety of your protein sources and, if you're eating them regularly you'll get the full complement of essential amino acids.

Amino acids are the building blocks of proteins and are essential to our growth and good health and I talk about them in the next section.

Protein Digestion, Preserving Nutrients, Raw And Cooked ...

Essentially you want to consume foods that collectively will provide the full array of amino acids. You will find your amino acids in foods that are not made entirely of protein (they also have fats and carbohydrates). Keep in mind that there really are only a handful of 100% protein foods. They are all processed to some degree and include egg whites, boiled shrimp, non-fat cottage cheese and fat-free turkey breast.

Eggs, which have no carbs, are only pure protein if you don't eat the yolk. Fish is low in carbohydrate but not devoid of them. It's clear that none of these foods can form the mainstay of a healthy diet. And incidentally, none of them will make it into any of your green smoothies!

All nutritious foods have a complex profile of ingredients. It's we as humans who try to categorize them so they can fit into boxes. You'll be dismissing and including foods on your smoothie inclusion list based on nutritional value and their ability to blend well.

Many foods that are considered 'carbohydrates' have significant proportions of protein in them. Take raw spinach. Thanks to Popeye most people will know that spinach has a high amount of protein. According to www.nutritiondata.self.com it has 56% carbs and 30% protein. Broccoli has 64% carbs and 26% protein.

Chia seeds are regarded as a high source of protein (36% carbs, 53% fats and 11% protein) and more importantly they are a source of all the essential amino acids (complete protein).

While we're on that point, there are definitely certain foods that lend themselves to smoothie-ing and others that don't. I recommend you don't let dogmatic food combining principles based solely on numbers or calorie counting get in the way of logic and a nutritious smoothie.

Don't Overthink Your Nutrition

I'd like you to simplify your approach to your decision-making when it comes to food. Go for a variety of high nutrient foods. Don't bamboozle yourself with percentages of what's in them. How could you possibly keep track? And how can we as humble humans understand the complexity of their interactions beyond scientific data (which in itself is just an interpretation)?

Concern yourself with acquiring the best quality food, organic or pesticide-free if you can manage it and eat a range or complement of different things. If you're vegan and vegetarian know enough about where to get all your essential amino acids, your essential fatty acids in the right proportions across your diets, your iron and your vitamin B12. That's just common sense and about your healthy survival.

And, no matter who you are, drink at least 2 liters of water every day and consume good quality sea salt.

Keeping Your Proteins Available For Use

High protein foods such as meat and eggs may not be as useful as you would like because they are normally cooked. There is a ton of information about proteins freely available online. Raw food 'experts' say that raw protein is the best because uncooked protein is of a higher quality. They suggest that cooking destroys upwards of 50% of the protein contained within food by denaturing the proteins.

Other sources say that in order to digest protein it needs to be denatured to make amino acids bioavailable. It really is hard to wade through the information and misinformation and decide which is which.

Try this on for size and practicality. Denaturing is going to happen anyway. In actual fact, **it's the viability of amino acids that you want to preserve**. Certain cooking processes do destroy certain amino acids, particularly with high heat and burning (such as barbecues).

So what do we do with this information?

You do know one thing for sure, **you do preserve more nutrients such as vitamins and enzymes when the temperatures are lower**. My personal recommendation (without being dogmatic!) is to reduce the overall proportion of cooked food. Eat more raw food and make your way towards consuming eventually at least 80% raw food if you can help it! Green smoothies will shift the balance for you.

The (Scientific And Practical) Skinny On Proteins

Getting a little scientific here, it's important to know that:

- There are 20 amino acids that make up proteins

- Nine (9) of these are called *essential amino acids* (certain others are essential in certain circumstances)

- The body cannot manufacture essential amino acids so you need to find them in your diet

- You need a diet that has the building blocks of your proteins across all your food choices and across your meals

- You can find the right proportion of amino acids by eating well over time. It is a myth that you have to eat 'complete proteins' (proteins that have the essential amino acids in specific proportions) at EVERY meal. This is no longer considered critical. You DO need to eat well and ingest the building blocks over the course of a day or 2 or 3!

- Varying your foods; fruit, vegetables and greens and choosing your foods wisely will give you plenty of protein, even if you never eat any animal flesh.

If you're looking to put on muscle bulk then exercise and a good wholesome diet are your friends! Some of the best building blocks are not surprisingly, going to be found within the pages of this book AND when you use sound judgment in your food choices. Movement towards a high proportion of uncooked, organic (if possible) plant-based foods is one of the best health decisions you will ever make for you and your family.

How Much Of My Smoothie Should Be Green?

Somewhere at some time somebody made an arbitrary comment. They decided that the definition of a green smoothie is 40% greens, 50% fruit and 10% fat. I have also read it should be 60% fruit, 40% green leafy vegetables. Nowhere ANYWHERE can I ever find whether this is by volume or mass. And it cannot account for the fact that fats are in greens and fruit. So do you add extra fat?

For example certain green smoothie aficionados say 40% green leafy vegetables but then may only pop in 2 cups of leaves which weigh a small proportion of the smoothie. You'd have to put a HUGE volume of chickweed into a smoothie to reach that 40% and you'd need a much smaller amount if you were using, say, the heavier green, bok choy.

Well, I don't know about you, but that 'definition' is pretty unclear (and perhaps even a little misleading). Some greens are feather light. Others are dense.

Optimize Your Greens

Here's why it is probably better to think about optimizing your greens intake. I can tell you quite definitively that when you make a green smoothie you are not going to be placing a cupful of fruit and then its weight in greens to go along with it. One cup of fruit can weigh hundreds of grams.

For the purposes of testing the so-called formula for green smoothies (and to have a little fun) I did some experimenting of my own. I weighed the pineapple and papaya in my smoothie and it was about 500 grams. The leaves I put in (2 whole packed cups) weighed around 150 grams.

In that smoothie, the percentage was about 77% fruit, 23% greens. If I had used bok choy it would have been in the vicinity of 350-400 grams. So the proportions of fruit would be 55-59% and the greens would be 45-41%. (That's closer.)

In another smoothie, fruit weighing 340g along with 2 cups of chickweed at 120g makes the proportion of fruits very high at 74% fruit with only 26% greens.

The bottom line is this: The proportion is going to depend on your ingredients. Pure and simple.

In my opinion, it strains credibility to claim definitive proportions. A heavy fruit will shift the balance away from the 40% of greens. The salad type leaves are very light in mass. So instead I have consistently added at least 2 (well-packed) cups of greens to every smoothie.

Let's just put all that to bed and say: "We get it". Cram a lot of greens into a smoothie and if you balance that with other well-chosen ingredients you're sure to get a highly nutritious drink. Job's done. The percentages are just an indication that you need greens. By the way, if, in the beginning, you can't do that in a smoothie, then eat a few salads.

Ingredient Quantities In This Book

My aim is to make these recipes easy to make. I have read many recipes over the decades that suggest using a bunch of this or that. A bunch? Sorry, that does NOT compute. Sometimes bunches of say, basil are just a couple of stems with a few dozen leaves. While at other times a bunch is a veritable bounty of literally hundreds of the fresh green fragrant herb.

Or what about when you read something like 'a small pineapple'? I live in pineapple country. I can find pineapples that would yield less than 1 cup and other ones that you could get over 2 cups out of and both of which you COULD consider small. So ...

Instead of telling you a bunch of basil, you're more likely to be told a quantity. You'll see '1/2 cup basil' or '1 cup of pineapple'.

Handfuls, Bunches Or Cups?

You won't be told to throw in a ¼ 'bunch' of basil. There is the very occasional handful (of nuts or mint). Smoothie-ing is not an exact science because the produce you buy is variable. However it is easy to measure a cupful of greens or fruit.

In this book you'll find that I have included a simple and as accurately-reproducible guide to measuring ingredient quantities as I could manage.

While fruit sizes can change, where it matters I have quantified it for you.

Which Vegetables Are Starchy?

I agree with many other smoothie greats (!) that starchy vegetables should be avoided in smoothies. If you need proof of that, then try to imagine a potato smoothie. Hahaha

There are degrees however. Some will tell you not to put in beets (beetroot) or carrots because they are too high in carbs or even starchy. They say it's because it needs to sit within the guidelines of a combination diet.

So to make it easy, how about I give you a quick guide on starchy and non-starchy veggies (at least the ones that are sometimes in contention!)?

Starchy Vegetables To Be Avoided In A Green Smoothie

Don't put these in your smoothie:

- Corn, squash and pumpkin, potatoes and sweet potatoes, peas and parsnips.

You will see that in this book that I often love to use the *leaves* of the sweet potato. They are very mild and blend well. They're also high in iron. :)

Non-Starchy Vegetables

There are plenty of non-starchy vegetables. Let me AVOID making this a long list, because frankly, common sense tells you that you'll want to avoid putting eggplant or mushrooms in your smoothies!

Instead I have listed the vegetables that go very well in green smoothies *for their nutritional profile* and the way they complement the other ingredients. Some of these vegetables will have a tiny amount of starch in them.

Nature really does things in a way that does not necessarily 'comply' with man-made rules. Trust me, these vegetables work *really* well in a green smoothie! (I should know – I tested every single one of them!)

- Carrots, beets, broccoli, celery, onion, tomato and peppers and cucumbers (those last three are technically fruits) and of course just about all your 'green leafies'.

I've made sure that the recipes in this book reflect the best way to give a good blend and flavor.

Not All Green Smoothies Are Green

Well ... they are and they aren't. To me, a green smoothie is all about putting lots of green leafy vegetables into a well-assimilated good-

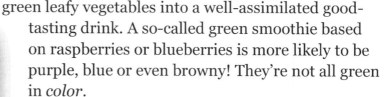

tasting drink. A so-called green smoothie based on raspberries or blueberries is more likely to be purple, blue or even browny! They're not all green in *color*.

In fact I have enjoyed smoothies of colors of a wide spectrum from yellowy lime, to vivid green, to dark green, browns, purples and reds! A veritable smoothie rainbow.

The key is to have a couple of cups of green leaves (that are well packed) in each serving! The amount may increase or decrease because there are other green vegies that you may add that are beneficial.

For example if I am adding a stalk of celery, then the recipe may just call for 1-1.5 cups of greens. If I am adding herbs such as cilantro (coriander) or mint or parsley they may just add to the amount of greens.

I often substitute a ¼ to a ½ cup of broccoli florets. A recipe may ask you to add in a handful of sprouts.

Our Obsession With Food And The 'Best Way To Cook It'!

The world seems to revolve on the joy and fun of putting ingredients together. "Masterchef" style television shows pitting cooking prowess skills of amateurs head to head. Sometimes it seems the more detailed and the more steps you put food through, the more revered the result will be.

It's great news that there is a movement against the scarily growing fast-food lifestyle. It's not at all large enough, if you ask me. It's going to take quite some time before the results of any healthy changes are obvious in our western cultures.

Some people are now subscribing to a 'slow food' philosophy, taking their time in the preparation and eating of their fare.

Probably the most popular new(ish) food movement is the Raw Food Movement!

Raw Food You Ask?

I do LOVE raw food and I do also eat amounts of cooked food. Eating raw food, as my family does in increasing amounts, is not only delicious it makes us feel vibrant, energetic and healthy.

But with children, unless you've started out with superlative habits, convincing your child(ren) that MOSTLY raw food is the way to go can be downright challenging.

There is a tremendous amount of evidence, both real and anecdotal which shows that plant-based foods and especially those that aren't cooked are the elixir of life. Ha, a bold claim. But frankly, we are talking some amazing effects on the human body.

Put simply: Green smoothies help you consume more raw foods – EFFORTLESSLY!

In almost every case plant-based and raw foods have more nutrients for your system. In other words the body has a greater chance of assimilating all the goodness in the food. You see, cooking processes that use heat above about 115 degrees Fahrenheit (c 46 degrees Celsius) are responsible for making changes in the nutrients, often completely inactivating them.

There also seems to be quite a backlash against the mis-information that we are constantly fed by the big wheels of business; pharmaceutical, marketing, food companies and governments.

People (once they've had some kind of awakening) want to return to the simplicity of wholefoods, natural medicine, or even better, using food as the first port of call for healing conditions and diseases and in doing so maintaining health.

Ah yes! Raw food. It does seem logical that eating fresh fruit and vegetables in their raw uncooked state in most cases is going to deliver the cleanest, most nutritious form of nourishment for the body and soul!

Contrast that with those recipes designed to hide ground up vegetables in cooked meals to trick the children. Zucchini cake - I mean, really? Delicious, maybe, but what purpose does it serve (in most cases) but to subdue people into a false sense of security.

Most often the nutrition has, in all intents and purposes completely left its origin and that vegetable has now just become a 'filler'. And pssst I have been guilty of disguising vegies in certain meals. Fortunately with green smoothies, it's just easier and there's nothing to hide – and the nutrition is there. It's a win-win-win situation.

I am not a raw food evangelist and this book is not at all political.

Raw Food Waiver

I think it's worth issuing you a waiver here: While cooking food can kill enzymes and nullify the nutrition, there are foods which IF you choose to eat them, really MUST be cooked.

Some foods need to be cooked if they contain virulent (dangerous) bacteria or toxins. An example for you: You would never eat raw kidney beans. They can't even be simply added to a stew, they need to be boiled first to kill the phytotoxin or to bring it down to non-toxic levels.

Certain components of certain foods are more potent when they are cooked making them better for you. While tomatoes are great raw, if you want to improve your lycopene intake (a potent antioxidant) then cooking improves lycopene levels.

Cooking carrots has often been recommended so that the cell walls can breakdown effectively and therefore release nutritional goodness. Cooking is also said to increase their level of beta-carotene (which converts to vitamin A). Cooking does however destroy levels of vitamin C.

In certain parts of the world people are being cautioned not to eat raw eggs, meat and even sprouts because of certain microorganisms.

If you pulverize your carrots in a blender or a juicer then you'll get everything you need in very good amounts. Much of the work is done by your machine. The cell walls get broken down effectively and the nutritional wonder inside becomes more bioavailable.

From an ease of digestion standpoint cooking your carrots is good (especially boiled whole) because I can probably bet that you're not chewing or pulverizing them in their raw form as well as your blender or juicer can. With the current juicing and smoothie-making trends you don't need to cook them. Raw is my preference.

Tuning Into You

When you consume your green smoothies you will notice a change in your relationship to food (if you haven't already). It feels so empowering to reject old food choices easily and naturally while preferring things you may have even felt ambivalent or repulsed by before.

Case in point: I simply cannot imagine my daughter consistently sitting down to a plate of salad with 2 cupsful of green leaves along with a pile of other foods. It would seem a very daunting (and large) task. She now has AT LEAST that every time she has a smoothie. It feels like a victory to her parents, but to her, she feels empowered and happy to know she's easily contributing to a lasting legacy of health (deliciously).

The benefit is that, over a short amount of time, you really learn to tune into what your body really needs and wants. It responds so well to the clean fresh ingredients. You will find that choosing what you need becomes intuitively easier – without effort.

Isn't it time to welcome some ***Green Smoothie Magic*** into your life and into the lives of those around you? Especially kids. Here's your chance to deliver LARGE amounts of the most nutritious food available to you in a delicious and easy to drink fashion.

My little sister (and it's funny now that I am well into my 5th decade I can still call my sister little!) said to me when I told her I was writing a book about Green Smoothies: *"The idea of drinking lettuce makes me want to throw up."* But now her family has the same blender as mine, and we both compare Smoothie Magic Success interstate and over the phone.

Her very first experience was very funny. My own daughter Isabelle's favorite smoothie is one she gives the impossible score 311 out of 10! It has bananas, raspberries, greens and mint, vanilla, cinnamon and ice. Easy!

When my sister prepared one of her son's his first smoothie right in front of him, the sounds of disgust when he saw cupsful of baby spinach go in were to say the least amusing. Dominic rejected that particular smoothie! But what is funnier is that his first one was his own concoction of carrot, celery and apples, berries, banana and ice, which he loved.

~ • ~

Don't Get Stuck With The Same Green

You know what they say? Everything in moderation. There is some talk in 'smoothie world' that eating the same greens all the time is actually a way to become sick. The alkaloids in plants are nature's way of plant self-preservation and they form part of the plant's defense.

If you ate say, only baby spinach leaves in all your smoothies every day, every smoothie, then you run the risk of having what would be considered toxic levels of the specific alkaloids found in spinach.

There are different kinds of alkaloids and different effects. Rather than make this a scientific or scary subject, let's take the drama right out of it. The answer is simple. Don't ever just eat the same greens over and over again. Eat a variety.

To make it super simple I will provide you with list of green leafy vegetables. You won't need to lock yourself into one green for any particular green smoothie. I will give you suggestions that will give the same results!

When I give you a recipe with 2 cups of green leaves – then feel free to make up your 2 cups of greens out of one of the lists. Say for example you are making my Vanilla Pudding Smoothie! You definitely won't want to be choosing any sharp tasting greens. You wouldn't choose Arugula (Rocket) or Watercress.

Instead you'll choose from the following: Asparagus Lettuce, Baby Spinach, Chickweed, Tatsoi, Pak Choy, Bok Choy, Sweet Potato Greens. Mid tasting ones can be Kale, Chard depending on the variety. Maybe you've heard of Purslane, Lambsquarter, Romaine or Cos, Beet Greens, Carrot Greens. Stay tuned for a long list of greens.

Knowing Your Greens – Substituting For Holistic Nutrition

I know you'll always find some greens in your supermarket or local store. You'll also find greens at your local market. Of course buying freshly picked produce is always better. In my opinion I would always prefer organic produce. Sometimes however it is availability and financial considerations that determine what you do buy.

Make sure you find a variety of greens. Taste them all. Farmers' markets are great for asking stallholders if you can taste a leaf or two of varieties you are unfamiliar with. Get familiar with what kinds of greens are mild, medium and strong. When you find a recipe I will often specify a particular green to use.

However, if you for example, cannot find Bok Choy then substitute a different mild green. The taste will be substantially similar and perhaps identical.

By the same token, if that smoothie with Bok Choy in the ingredients list is your all-time favorite concoction and you drink it several times per week then substituting other mild greens will ensure that you have a good complement of nutrients in your diet (and you won't over-ingest those particular alkaloids).

Substituting greens will give you wonderful freedom in your smoothie preparations.

Seasonal Greens

In winter, the range of greens available is naturally much smaller. Winter greens are high in vitamin A. Enjoy including Kale, Collard Greens, Chard, Spinach and even Mustard Greens (careful they are spicy).

You'll find Arugula (Rocket) and even Turnip Greens can be used. Use Beet Greens, Carrot tops and Winter Purslane. You'll find Endive and other Chicory varieties (also a little strong or bitter), Cabbage and if it's not too cold, Mizuna lettuce.

In summer you'll find many different lettuce varieties thrive. You'll find the tight head of Iceberg, the loose leaf varieties include Red Oak Leaf and Butter Lettuce, and other 'fancy' lettuce. Romaine (or Cos) has an elongated head. Happily, you'll still find the winter greens above.

The list of all greens is very long. I have included many in the next section Remember to visit any local markets to see what's actually in season or grown fresh locally.

Greens

In summary, go to your market and taste different greens. If they're mild then feel free to substitute for any recipes that specify mild greens. If they are more bitter or pungent then substitute them for greens in recipes that specify stronger greens.

The key is to create a balance in your eating. Do NOT rely on all baby spinach to the exclusion of every other green. Have a selection of washed and carefully stored greens. Know which ones are mild or strong.

Mix And Match

When the recipe says 2 cups of mild greens, reach into a single bag for 2 cups of greens for a single green smoothie, or take a cupful of 2 different varieties. The taste won't be that different between the mild leaves.

For example, I will often use the following when making a green smoothie with 2 cups of greens: asparagus lettuce and sweet potato leaves, different choy varieties, cabbage and sweet potato leaves, chickweed and spinach. The list goes on because the combinations are endless.

So, when it comes to greens, the world is your (vegetarian) oyster. Put your greens on rotation, do some experimenting.

A List Of Mild Greens

As you can see, you will be spoiled for choice. I surveyed green smoothie makers (the people!) and found that they felt restricted by recipes that said that they needed to use chickweed or lambsquarters. They told me that if a recipe recommends a particular green then that's the one they feel they have to use.

I've taken a *different* approach that you'll love! **My recipes give you the freedom to mix and match your greens** in the way that suits you. You could buy a variety of greens and use whatever you want depending on whether the smoothie recipe you decide to make is better with 2 cups mild greens, 2 cups strong greens or even 1 cup of each.

Here's a list of mild greens. I am sure you'll find plenty that will fit your needs.

- baby spinach
- bok or pak choy or gay choy
- sweet potato leaves
- pumpkin leaves
- papaya leaves
- chickweed
- asparagus lettuce
- kale (smaller leaves can be milder than large ones) comes in many varieties and some are mild and others could be considered stronger.
- tatsoi lettuce
- chard (same group as spinach and similar in taste)
- collard greens
- carrot greens
- beet greens (similar to spinach in taste)
- cabbage
- mizuna
- butter lettuce
- wandering jew
- romaine or cos lettuce
- purslane (similar to spinach in taste)
- pigweed (similar to spinach)
- lambsquarter (similar to spinach in taste)
- amaranth
- marsh mallow
- alfalfa sprouts
- broccoli sprouts
- lentil sprouts
- mung bean sprouts

- sunflower sprouts and sprouts from garbanzo beans (chick peas), lentils, buckwheat, soybeans (edamame), quinoa, fenugreek, peas, barley, oats, millet and wheat

- and so on

So for example, if a recipe calls for 2 cups of mild greens I could easily add 1 cup of bok choy and 1 of sweet potato leaves, or 1 cup kale and tatsoi. You get the picture.

A List Of Stronger Greens

For stronger greens I will use

- rocket

- watercress

- endive (can be bitter)

- mustard greens (can vary in their spiciness to be VERY peppery)

- dandelion greens

- radish tops

- radicchio

- radish, mustard, onion, chive and other hot sprouts

- sorrel (not bitter but in the strong list due to its pronounced lemony flavor)

Remember, find your supplier at your markets or local store and get to know your greens.

Try Before You Take The Plunge

You know, sometimes you can buy rocket, watercress, mustard greens or other strong greens that are anywhere from mildly spicy to peppery to downright bitter. It's a good idea to taste test them before you go sticking 2 big cupsful into a smoothie. Mind you, you will be very pleasantly surprised how well strong greens go in some quite sweet smoothies.

Our daughter wouldn't dream of eating a salad with rocket in it, but happily slurps down an entire smoothie with 2 cups of the stuff when it's accompanied by mango and mint.

Don't be afraid to put them in. But if you taste a particularly strong batch of greens, put anywhere from one handful to one cup in instead of 2 cups. Make up the difference with a cup of mild greens and it will all 'even out in the wash'.

Can't Find Chickweed? Don't Know What It Is?

You see, you may live in a part of the world where you can't find chickweed. You can go to the substitution list and choose something that will give you the same effect.

Where you live and the season you're experiencing will also determine what greens you'll find.

Maybe you're in a part of the country where you have an incredibly wide range of sprouts and leaves. Get to know the different types by taking them home and testing them.

If, on the other hand, you're somewhere that's not so much on the frontier of healthy eating, then perhaps you're only going to find basics such as Baby Spinach, Kale, Silverbeet and Romaine lettuce. Maybe you'll start to grow your own different varieties.

Lambsquarter? Pigweed? Purslane? Goosefoot? Fat-Hen? Yikes!

OK, OK! So you've read other recipes elsewhere that make claims as to the better varieties of greens and that some are more magical than others. The truth is that this may indeed be true. When it comes to the names above I can tell you that there is some confusion even to which one is called what!

So, here's my advice. You will only have access to a certain number of greens. That number will be more limited if you only ever to go your average commercial supermarket or outlet. If you go to a farmers' market then you may have more from which to choose. You may choose to grow certain varieties yourself.

The Art Of Following Recipes: Two Types Of People

There are 2 types of people in this world when it comes to following a recipe:

1. Those that MUST have everything in that recipe list to the letter; and

2. Those that intuitively know how to improvise.

I want to take the hassle and stress out of having to have precise and particular greens AND give you the joy and freedom to add in nutrition and variety without having a significant effect on the taste outcome of your **Green Smoothie Magic** experience!

So let's get started with some great recipes. Remember, what's delicious to me may appear slightly differently on your own taste scale. That's life. I have tested these smoothies with many people, including my 9 year old!

Some of the smoothies that I think are amazing I get agreement from everyone. Others that I think are so-so get a 10 out of 10 with smoothie skeptics. While with others it's the other way around.

All in all I have given a range of flavors and consistencies with palatable and yes, delicious tastes and effects. Some are light and fresh and tangy. Others are smooth, luxuriant, sweet and creamy. Others have a citrus note, others taste more herb-laden.

You'll start to tune into what works best for you and sometimes it just won't matter how it tastes, it will be how you FEEL after having something so healthful and life-giving!

Choosing Your Greens: A Quick Primer

Here's what you need to do:

1. Taste what is available to you

2. Determine if it's mild, medium or strong in its taste and

3. Vary your intake. Remember not to take only one or two varieties of greens.

4. Have several in your refrigerator each week. Vary from week to week so you can purchase significant amounts of say, 4 types rather than small amounts of say 8 varieties

Storage And Use For Smoothies

In my mind it's best to have everything EASY to find and use. You will see that I recommend washing, drying and storing your greens so that they're accessible at a moment's notice. You want everything to be as easy as it can be. That will continue to inspire you to further success and even more vibrant health. It will keep you on track to make good decisions too (rather than reaching for the 'wrong' stuff!).

Below you'll see some suggestions. If you prefer other ways then go with that.

TIP: Wash Your Greens As Soon As You Get Home!

I believe you need to set yourself up for success! I have found that an invaluable thing to do is to wash your greens when you bring them home (or in from the garden). Fill up the kitchen sink so that the leaves you have float.

Remove the twist ties or rubber bands or other packaging from your greens.

Cut off the roots of plants that you don't need or intend to use. Separate whatever leaves need separating from the stem. Clean the dirt off. Check for little bugs because they do hide in there especially if you buy organic produce.

Other Essentials

Maybe your first step has been to actually buy this and perhaps other smoothie books and other items that inspire you to great health. Other essentials are a blender, a good knife and a chopping board. Consider other items that could inspire you including juicers, books, eBooks, a special knife or maybe some new glassware for your smoothies.

Bare minimum: You need recipes, knife, blender and your produce.

Drying Your Greens

Use a colander to strain most of the water from your leaves. If this is all you did and put them in the fridge your greens would still perish. ***Drying them well is essential.*** So drain them and then move them from the colander to a clean dry tea towel that you lay out on a bench, table or in a bowl. You can pat the leaves dry. If you have a salad spinner this is very useful.

While it can be time consuming, it's well worth the effort to spend the time to process your greens straight away. It really is a joy to get your washed and dried greens out of the fridge and pop them straight into the blender.

Storing Your Greens

Place the greens into bags or boxes. When you do, place either a tea towel or some kitchen paper on which to sit your greens so that condensation is mopped up and the greens have less contact with the plastic (which can cause some spoiling).

Stems

You don't need to discard the stems. Many recipes will tell you to only use the coriander leaves (cilantro). With green smoothies, you get to use more of the plant.

Enjoy using more of your parsley, coriander and even mint. Simply avoid using the very woody stems as thick and fibrous green stems won't blend well.

Some people believe that the stems have least nutrition. This is not the case. However, they do have more fiber and for that reason may be less enjoyable in salads. The upside is they are an excellent source of flavor and fiber for your smoothies.

Herbs In Water

Maybe you want to store your bunches of herbs upright in a glass or cup with the roots or cut stems covered with water. You can do that in the fridge covered with a bag however I could never fit much else in my fridge so I prefer to wash them. Besides you'll use these things often.

The other way to store your herbs is again, in a cup or container and then leave them to enjoy the fresh air on your kitchen bench top. Keep them out of strong direct sunlight if possible so that they last longer. You would probably have to wash them as you need them.

Of course you can grow pots of herbs in or near your kitchen. It's glorious to have access to a basil or coriander plant right there at your fingertips. It's a great alternative too, for people in apartments with little or no garden or just a balcony.

Different Ingredients Add To Your Health And Help Weight Loss

You may be here reading this because you want to lose weight or trim some shape. You will notice that some smoothies have nuts in them. These provide taste, texture and yes, fat. The vitamins you need in your whole diet are water and fat soluble.

You need fats in your diet. They are essential for your hormonal (and other) systems to thrive. There are 4 fat-soluble vitamins: A, D, E and K. So feel confident that inclusion of obviously more fatty ingredients are as valuable to you as the other ones! Besides most foods have some amount of fats in them. It's the quality of fat that you're looking to include by adding nuts and seeds.

In eating a balanced diet you need a good range of fats. You need them for nerve function, for vitamin absorption, to keep creating healthy cells and a healthy immune system. The right fats will help lower cholesterol and decrease risk of heart attacks.

There are fats in your fruit and vegetables but you may not get all the fatty acids (particularly omega-3) you need without getting them from sources such as nuts, seeds, legumes and good quality non-hydrogenated plant oils.

For example you'll find monounsaturated fats (they're good) in almonds, hazelnuts, macadamias and brazils. You'll find omega 3 in chia seeds, flaxseeds, flaxseed oil, walnuts and walnut oil, pumpkin seeds and oil. Good all-rounder candidates which provide poly and monounsaturated fats are brazil nuts, sunflower, pumpkin and sesame seeds (and their oils of course).

While you can find omega-3 fats in fish, you are probably not going to make any fish smoothies!

How 'Green' Should My First Smoothies Be?

Some people recommend starting very low on the green scale (by maybe throwing in just a tiny amount of greens) and work their way up. If you have a smoothie skeptic in the house then this may or may NOT be necessary. Just make sure you start with something that you're SURE they'll love.

That's why I gave my daughter raspberry and banana. I didn't need to start on low greens. It was so yummy she's been happy to try anything ever since.

I have friends who will drink a smoothie regardless of the taste because they just KNOW that it's good for them. If a smoothie is just halfway palatable that's good enough for them. I can get through a not-so-delicious smoothie once in a while. Taste *with* nutrition is the ultimate aim.

Green Smoothie Magic Basics

Every smoothie recipe is going to have significant green content! As I have hinted at elsewhere, I have tried in most if not all cases to put at least 2 cupsful of green leafy vegetables. This may include celery or broccoli.

Oftentimes you'll find quite a bit more than 2 cups especially when you add herbs. You will find smoothies just with greens as the base, with greens and herbs (yep, that's right, more greens) broccoli florets and other items that add to the 2 cup minimum.

Every smoothie is going to need some fluid added to it. That will be in the form of:

- Water

- Ice

- Nut milk or even nuts and water (I will explain the difference between these 2 similar ingredients later)

- Coconut water

- Seed milk or seeds and water

- Oranges and other juicy items such as celery which will likely reduce the amount of separately added fluid comparatively

When you do add fluid, you'll always be safe adding just plain (filtered if you have it) water. You can optionally add coconut water or you can add nut milks. As I mentioned above you can also use nut milk or nuts and water.

Should I Add Nut Milk Or Nuts?

In writing this book I found that I have had extraordinary results with using nuts. I am a practical kind of gal! I know that there will be MANY people out there and perhaps you're one of them, that neither has the time nor the inclination to make a liter of nut milk as yet another step in the process.

Making nut milk usually entails putting nuts or seeds (soaked or not) into a blender, adding water and processing. After the nuts or seeds are pulverized and your milk is ready the nut milk is separated from the pulp through a piece of material (muslin) or a nut milk bag.

Although simple it does a) introduce another thing to do and b) takes the pulp away which still has nutritional value.

I experimented with using a handful of nuts in the blender with a cup of water first. In blending the nuts or seeds first you are able to make your nut milk first so that it's lovely and smooth and then continue blending your smoothie by adding the other ingredients in your recipe at this stage.

In this way you keep ALL the nutrition and your improve the consistency. By the way you can soak those nuts first if you wish. (See the next section about soaking).

If you have a really good blender you may not even need to make the milk first prior to adding the other ingredients. In any case, for the sake of simplicity I will often split recipes into stages so that you can get a smooth finish.

Unlock The Living Magic

Did you know that there is a way to potentially unlock the living magic inside every nut and seed? You may have heard of recipes that ask you to soak nuts before you use them.

Why Soak The Nuts?

Have you ever noticed how a bowl of almonds can stay on your table for literally weeks or months and they can still taste fresh? Well, that's the 'enzyme inhibitors' at work. Those little miracles will keep the nut from sprouting until the conditions are right.

Is Soaking Necessary?

When you soak the nuts for a recipe then you are getting rid of enzyme inhibitors. This means your food transforms itself from a latent life-on-hold scenario to one that is brimming with life's potential and full of activated growth enzymes. Sometimes, too, the nuts taste better and any bitter taste can disappear. They blend better as well.

How To Soak Nuts

Cover the nuts with water. Allow them to soak. Almonds and macadamias should be soaked overnight. Cashews, walnuts and pecans need much less time – about 2 hours. Sunflower seeds can be soaked from 30 minutes to 2 hours.

Making It Easy For You

Look I have made it a little easy for you! A handful of soaked nuts and water in a smoothie, well blended will provide both the milk base and thickener in one easy step*, AND you get the nutrition from the pulp.

You may not be one to make your own nut milks. Just because I do it doesn't mean you have to. In fact now that we have smoothies every day we just have some soaked nuts on hand. I have found that simply throwing in the nuts and seeds this way is an excellent alternative. You just have to measure the amounts. That's easy!

* The better your blender, the easier this is! Saves time too :)

Cyanide Anyone?

There are certain foods that contain cyanide that you may be eating from time to time. The technical term is: Cyanogenic glycosides. In small amounts it is OK. Cyanide is a poison. The one food that we encounter with the potential ability to form free hydrogen cyanide is the bitter almond. Apparently it's the bitter almonds that have the most glycosides.

By the way 'sweet almonds' are very low in cyanogenic properties. Sweet almonds are great for smoothies and almond milk. Some almonds have none of these toxic compounds. It's comforting to know that only sweet almonds are grown commercially.

You will also find cyanogenic glycosides in apple seeds and apricot pits. A small amount of apricot seeds are said to contribute to your good health as they are a source of vitamin B17. I don't include apricot kernels in any recipe but you are welcome to add them optionally to a smoothie here and there!

As for apple seeds, including in a smoothie from time to time is fine. Eating apple seeds accidentally in a smoothie if done occasionally poses no risk (according to my research) and it's not necessary to avoid them. You need a LOT of apple seeds to create a toxic situation. You would need many handfuls of them. Apple seeds are said to contain vitamin B17 as well. The jury's out on their anti-cancer role.

Cut out your seeds if you feel concerned.

The risk of cyanogenic glycosides in commercially available almonds is very low (even though some bitter almonds can be part of a sweet almond harvest). The good news is that soaking almonds and apricot kernels reduces the amount of cyanogenic glycoside content.

Don't be alarmed. The main reason you will soak your almonds in any case is to remove the 'enzyme inhibitors'. The side benefit is, that if there are any cyanogenic compounds in there even that amount will lessen.

So, soak your almonds (and your apricot kernels). Soaking overnight is best. Then discard the soak water and rinse well. If you don't have the time and particularly want to use unsoaked almonds from time to time that will be fine too. Just use a maximum ¼ cup of the nut per smoothie.

It will give you the taste and texture you're after. Almonds as you may remember are a wonderful source of calcium. Remember you can use other nuts too.

Using Nuts To Make Milk

You will find a number of recipes that use nuts or nut milk, and other ways to add fluid that are neither water nor dairy.

Substitutions

Here are some hints and tips for you so that you can substitute different ingredients to make your recipes adaptable.

Nut Substitution

Some ideas for you:

- If you have allergies to ingredients on a recipe list then make a substitution. Perhaps you will use sesame seeds, sunflower seeds, a different nut, coconut water instead.

- Don't want to use, or don't have nut or coconut milk? Choose water.

- Don't have nuts handy to make your own? Use packaged nut milk or rice milk or oat milk.

- Want to use dairy milk? That's your choice. I personally don't like to do that with smoothies. If you're after vibrant health or weight loss, it is my belief that there are much better choices than using cow's milk.

Fruit Substitutions

Feel free to change up the ingredients of any recipe. The result will be different but you can change things to give the same effect. Here are just a handful of suggestions:

- Substitute nectarine for peach either as fresh or dried.

- Use apple or kiwi or pineapple interchangeably.

- Grapes are a good substitute for apples or pears. Just make sure they are seedless.

- For a smooth consistency you may try interchanging banana, mango, young coconut flesh or avocado.

- Change out dates and use different dried fruit, or add a sweet fresh fruit such as a pear, banana or mango.

It's Your Smoothie, So You Choose The Thickness

In every smoothie you will add some liquid. Generally I have deliberately underplayed the amount of liquid you can add. This way you'll be able to create the smoothie of the perfect consistency *for you*. It's easy to add more fluid.

Icy, Cold Or Just Room Temperature

I have a preference for cold (but not icy) green smoothies.

You'll notice that I add ice on the ingredients list on every smoothie. How much you add is up to you and it depends on what you put in in the first place. Let me explain.

When you add your fruit you may be adding fruit from a bowl on the bench, fruit from the fridge or even the freezer. The thickness and temperature of your green smoothie will change depending on the nature of the ingredients you put in.

Naturally, the more warm or fridge-temperature fruit and vegetables you add, the warmer it will be. In just about every case the recipe will call for you to start by adding only one cup of water.

It is at that stage that you can test the thickness and temperature. If the temperature is too warm and it's too thick then simply adding ice usually does the trick.

If you're adding frozen fruit the result will of course be different. Maybe you'll have added a frozen banana or a cup of frozen mango (or even both). In this case you may only want to add water if it needs it.

Rule Of Thumb For Adding Ice And Water

Generally if you've only used fridge or bench temperature fruit you'll add ½ to 1 cup of ice. If you've used only frozen fruit you'll probably add some water, ice optional.

Add ice and water depending on whether you prefer thick or thin, room temp, cold or icy. Smoothies can thicken (and sometimes separate into layers) over time if left sitting. You'll probably want to give it a quick stir and decide if you need more water or ice.

It's easy to change the consistency and customize your smoothie! You'll be a specialist in no time. You'll learn that a thinner lighter smoothie can thicken up quite beautifully with a big cup or more of ice. It makes it kind of half smoothie half granita. Perfectly refreshing!

The Pragmatic Approach To Health, Nutrition And Everything!

In this section I want to debunk some myths and explain why you should not let fads – such as the 'superfood' fad –overly sway your decisions. I DO think some so-called 'superfoods' are great (while some are possibly a little marketing-hype) but I DON'T say your smoothies must have them!

So here you are. You want vibrant optimal health. Figuratively speaking you want your body to work like a well-oiled machine or to fire on all cylinders! You want all your systems to work in balance. You want all the food you ingest to actually promote your wellbeing.

In this information age you can find a lot of evidence to support whatever you want to look up. It is a well-known phenomenon that information in print form has a certain legitimacy. In other words if you read something, and especially if you read it often, you will more likely accept something as fact.

There are many health claims from the camps of Big Pharma, from the meat and dairy industries as well as the raw foodists. Who are you going to believe? It can be next to impossible to sort through all the information.

There are MANY claims that are on the internet that are unfounded. There are also many claims that are there simply because people find information, copy and paste it and voilà, it ends up being considered as fact, simply due to its popularity.

I recommend you develop critical thinking skills and be very careful not to accept everything you read just because you've read it a few times.

When it comes to health issues you want to take a pragmatic approach.

Will getting on the bandwagon and buying the latest greatest expensive sundried (but never above 108 degrees Fahrenheit) powdered fruit from the mountains of some South American country (which in order to purchase you need to take out another home loan) make a significant difference?

Maybe, maybe not.

What I can assure you though is that if you've been on anything that's similar to the S.A.D. (Standard American Diet) or you've been eating mainly cooked food and or processed food then it makes PERFECT SENSE that moving towards a diet that is FULL of fresh fruit and vegetables that are mostly raw and in their wholefood state, that are not processed IS going to make a significant difference. Period.

Taking extra superfoods like acai or camu camu or maca or whatever would just be a bonus. You can create the healthy you you want by sticking to the basic foods available so long as you have good variety.

Give It To Me Straight. What Are Superfoods?

One's definition of 'superfoods' is going to change depending on your beliefs.

In writing this book I had to examine my own beliefs. I had to examine what I was holding true and finding out on what I was basing those beliefs. When I write a book, I want to be responsible for publishing verifiable and reliable information.

I discovered much information from the raw foodists' camp that sounds as though it is full of fact. It's often hard to determine what is based on researched facts and studies and what is simply 'pseudo-science'. I found some information that is based on unsubstantiated claims and repeated information.

I also found that I myself had been guilty of repeating some of that information without ever having questioned or having searched for the facts.

Depending on where you look for this information say, about sprouts and microgreens, you will find completely conflicting information. And I mean polar opposite. This is definitely a time to question what you really believe and why.

Marketing is very persuasive. There are MANY new superfoods out there. It seems their panache and seductive powers can often have a LOT to do with the fact that you've not heard of them before.

This is just my opinion, but if you can't afford the expensive superfoods that you can find in many health food stores out there on the streets or in your computer then opt for the freshest, cleanest wholefoods that you can.

I have deliberately NOT added modern-day marketed superfoods to these recipes. You can add them to your heart's content. I want to make it EASY for you to find ingredients.

So for the sake of being ultra-pragmatic I believe you should not only eat loads and loads of raw fruit and vegetables but that you should also balance that with a small quantity of a variety of sprouts. More about sprouts and microgreens in a moment or two.

I also believe that you should use color as your guide. Make sure that you eat a wide variety of colorful foods. If you're only eating berries then you need to find green, yellow, paler colors and purple to balance it out. Make your plate (and your smoothie ingredients!) colorful and you will be on the right track.

My firm belief is that wholefoods beat processed foods hands down. *To rely only on expensive 'superfoods' that sound exotic, as the key to your health seems to me to be misguided.* **Start with the basics. Start with good organic or pesticide free, fresh local produce (do your best on as many counts as you can) and go from there.**

Superfoods Are Within Your Reach

Me? I believe that superfoods are everywhere. A superfood is really something that is nutritionally dense and contains higher than average amounts of nutrients such as vitamins, minerals, enzymes, fatty acids or amino acids.

If you have been eating store bought vegetables and fruit that have been treated with insecticides and selective herbicides and then cooked, perhaps your benefits will come from making the significant lifestyle change and eating raw organic vegetables in their whole form. Simple really.

Just making the switch from processed foods to wholefoods is your own move to superfoods. It's all relative. The change will really reflect the superfood qualities that you're after. The alchemy of ingredients of your unadulterated foods is definitely understated.

Furthermore, to call a couple dozen particular foods 'superfoods' may not actually be the belief you want to engender. Don't you think it would be better to consider all your well-chosen foods that you decide to put into your body as superfoods? That's the way I like to look at it.

You wouldn't call a jar of pasta sauce a superfood but you may like to think of traditionally grown fresh 'heirloom' tomatoes (ones that are grown from seeds passed down from generation to generation, naturally pollinated) organic garlic and basil (picked just this morning) in that way. Should you put some exotic sounding or difficult to pronounce substance on a pedestal?

The grass is not always greener over there!

Should You Eat Superfoods?

For the purposes of this section, we'll refer to the following foods, those often expensive and exclusive foods as 'superfoods'. We can refer to the humble rest as the simple miracles of nature. LOL!

As I implied before, to me an apple is a superfood. A beautiful fresh fruit, vegetable, green leafy, nut, seed and so on. They're all superfoods when you can eat them in their natural state and particularly when you can afford what seems to be in the modern age, the luxury of organic produce.

By the way, I have several smoothie recipes in the book that include using the wholefood raw (unroasted) cacao nibs. I am sure there are some out there who would say that it is one of those marketed superfoods. You would be right.

Let's consider that the cocoa powder that we've probably all bought over the years is actually a processed food. For the purposes of this book I will refer to cocoa as the processed product and cacao as the unprocessed one so that we can have some clarity. The alkalizing process they put cacao through to produce cocoa takes out the bitterness and contributes to a reduction in the nutrition.

Depending on the processing of the cocoa some will still maintain a reasonable nutritional profile while, if it is heavily processed, it will remove almost all the antioxidants that this superfood is known for.

Cacao is an unadulterated product from the cacao bean. The powder is just one of the products. It's been my experience in dozens of 'chocolate green smoothie' recipes that the bitterness of raw cacao powder can sometimes be overwhelming. For MANY testers it has been an acquired taste. Once they like it then they enjoy their choc green smoothie more.

However what I definitely found was that when I added raw cacao nibs to the smoothie (especially thrown in towards the end of blending) that they complement the flavor without overpowering the smoothie. You get to taste more of the ingredients. Plus you get a little extra 'mouth feel' component which I think is important for variety.

It becomes very same-old same-old if every smoothie you ever drink is well, um, too smooth :)

Here's a guide for you to add the OTHER 'superfoods' (and I will recap cacao too)!

The Superfoods In *Green Smoothie Magic*

Will I ask you to go out and buy lucuma or maca powder or mesquite? I think you realize that no, I won't! After all this book is penned so that you can make *Green Smoothie Magic* with easy to find ingredients!

If you're into 'superfoods' such as spirulina and other algaes, barley grass, wheatgrass, broccoli sprout powder, maca, lucuma, goji berries, acai berries, cacao, hemp, coconut, camu camu, bee products, noni and so on then do your research and make the purchase and then add it to whatever you like. But if you can't afford these 'superfoods' don't sweat it.

'Ordinary Ingredients' Have Magic Too

To call 2 dozen ingredients superfoods takes the focus from the life-giving properties of dozens and dozens of other wonderful foods that if treated well and remain relatively unprocessed also have extremely high merit. So don't forget the <u>supposedly</u> ordinary ingredients.

You may believe (as I do) that spirulina is well worth taking but you can't justify the expense of camu camu or lucuma. You may find some great benefits to your hormonal system taking maca powder but can't for the life of you find anything worth forking up the big bucks for some mesquite.

You may decide that coconut really is a miracle food (as many have attested) and you want to add some to your diet every day.

There are certain 'superfoods' that give you more value for your dollar. If you're considering more of nature's bounty as superfoods then you'll feel super (pardon the pun) when you add apples or almonds, broccoli and brazils, herbs and spices, berries and celery, dried fruits and leafy greens. Choose the best ingredients you can find within your budget.

So, Can You Put 'Superfoods' In Your Smoothies?

Heck yes! Why not, I say. Go ahead and add them in. My recipes are designed without needing any (sometimes prohibitively expensive) 'superfoods' because frankly there is still a LOT of contention about how much extra nutritional benefit one gets from these foods (above and beyond what you can get from other pure sources).

Use all my recipes as a base. Pop in some lucuma or maca or spirulina or acai or sprouted rice protein powder to your heart's content.

First make the smoothie and *then* add the extras that you want. The superfood will change the flavor somewhat. Maca for example, has a strong taste that is pretty hard to mask. It tastes a little bitter to me. Others will complement flavors very well. My '*Vanilla Pudding Smoothie*' or the '*Carob Pudding Smoothie*' will enjoy a little mesquite and or lucuma.

K.I.S.S.

Or you may decide to keep everything simple and just go for local organic with a good variety of nuts, seeds, fruit and vegetables. You will thrive no matter what, following the principles of eating a varied diet, mixing your greens avoiding just taking just say spinach and chard, but routinely picking from about a one and a half dozen different greens.

Me? I like to add spirulina to a smoothie now and then and I use coconut oil and yes I have a certain few 'trendy' superfoods but I NEVER go overboard. If you can afford it then test it all out. If you cannot then stick with the basics.

Cacao – Or How To Make A REAL Chocolate Smoothie (Yup, A Healthy One!)

One trendy well-promoted superfood that I actually believe is worth the trouble is cacao. It's the *unprocessed* form of cocoa (described above). I have done LOADS of testing and found that I can make great tasting smoothies that actually LOSE their delight for me when I add cacao powder.

Other people say "bring it on" and they add heaped tablespoons of the stuff. To me it imparts a strong and sometimes bitter taste to my smoothie. Don't get me wrong. I love cacao. But there IS a solution!

I have found that adding ¼ cup of cacao nibs made ALL the difference. Hey presto, wonderful chocolate smoothies that I believe are super-healthy. (Do your own experimenting.) I have put tasting notes along with a few recipes that have cacao nibs in them. You can use the powder if you like.

Generally though, if you're not used to the flavor then start with a smaller amount of cacao than the recommended quantity of nibs.

Spirulina And Other Sea Greens

Spirulina for example has a fantastic profile with all the essential amino acids, GLA (an essential omega-6 fatty acid and the only green in which it's found) works well in the gut to sustain healthy intestinal flora, has chlorophyll and beta-carotene, vitamin B (including B12 and folic acid, riboflavin and thiamine and more), magnesium, calcium, phosphorus, potassium and enzymes. I could go on!

You can choose to add a small amount of spirulina to any smoothie you wish.

Spirulina is a marvelous food and it does have a particular taste that may take some time to get used to. It could make a smoothie taste a little 'too green'. Blended in small amounts you will *'greenify'* your smoothie. Start with say, ¼ teaspoon (or less) and work your way up.

I have a very palatable mix of several greens together. My container (which I store in the fridge) has sea greens spirulina and chlorella along with barley grass and wheatgrass and then sweetened with some stevia.

Chia

If you were to break down chia seeds you would find a wealth of nutritional elements hidden in this plant food. I am not here to give you medical advice! However I can share with you some things I know about chia.

The jury is still out on how much chia one should include in one's diet. So, remember as with anything, vary your intake of different foods. Don't put chia into every single smoothie.

Remember for ANY nutritional profile to bear fruit (so to speak) those elements have to be bioavailable. It's no good saying that something is packed with protein to find out that none of it was digested in the body. Take a read and decide how you'll use chia. I use it from time to time (as part of my approach to a balanced food intake).

Chia seeds are very nutritious containing LOADS of omega 3 fatty acids. In fact they have been found to have the highest amount of these essential threes than any other plant. Amazingly it is also a "complete protein".

Now while you don't need complete proteins or their components every single meal (and as mentioned before, that theory is no longer accepted as correct) isn't it great to know that you can use a simple humble seed in your food that can provide you with a great nutritional profile?

The truly great thing about chia is that it has NO FLAVOR. With no taste that means you can add it to any smoothie recipe and reap the benefits! Yippeeeeeee

OK, back to where chia is at on the nutritional scale! As I said, it scores very highly when it comes to omega 3s. It also has large amounts of iron, magnesium and calcium. It has phosphorus, zinc and both soluble and insoluble dietary fiber. It has very high amounts of antioxidants too!

If you're vegetarian or vegan then it's very useful to know that you can get vitamin B12, Iron and Omega 3, folate and other essential dietary requirements in a neat little package. Hey, if you're an omnivore it's also useful to know! Ha! But those who are vegetarian or vegan do need to source their iron, B12 and Omega 3 particularly.

Here's the skinny on using chia. As I said, because it has no taste you can choose to put it in any smoothie. (Note, I didn't say that you should put it in *every* smoothie!)

Should You Add Chia Dry Or Soaked?

So, should you just add the seeds in from the packet? You can. And do so at a pinch. If you are able to soak your seeds beforehand then do that. They absorb somewhere between 7 and 12 times their own mass in water (some say more). They're very hydrating if you add them in to your smoothie presoaked.

They're also 'hydrophilic' (water-attracting) so they swell up and form a gel. This is why you'll see reference to 'chia gel'. Chia seeds have to draw moisture from somewhere. So let them do it before they're added to your smoothie if you can help it. That way you can use them to keep up your hydration levels.

Chia seeds add bulk and texture. Adding chia can create that smoothie texture. To make a thinner smoothie a little more 'smoothie-like' you could add a banana or mango or avocado if you are happy to change the flavor profile. Heap in a couple of tablespoons of soaked chia and one of 2 things will happen:

1. If you add them *after* you've finished blending, you'll end up with a nutritious 'bubble-tea'. In other words you'll have a smoothie with an interesting and enjoyable texture. It's important to have mouth feel in your smoothies and that they are not all just identically amorphous and smooth. Add some chia to vary your taste sensations. On that note you'll find that some smoothies have the added feel of seeds (think raspberry) cacao nibs or flax or shredded coconut.

2. Or you can add them in to the blend and pulverize them. You'll still benefit from improved consistency.

Should You Blend The Seeds?

Why blend them? You may have heard that chia is very high in protein. This is true. However *what you do to the seeds will determine the bioavailability of its entire nutritional profile.*

There has been at least 1 clinical study that has shown that if you consume chia seeds whole that the bioavailability of protein is around 25% of its content. Pulverize them, blend them in a smoothie and the ability to have the protein on hand (!) shoots way up to around 95%.

If you're choosing chia for its high nutritional profile then you do need to know there are effective and not-so-effective ways to get that 'stuff' into your system. Just throwing them in without blending may not do what you're after. Having the texture is very pleasing for some! Kids love that bubble-like sensation in the mouth.

Chia gel magic: Have some in your fridge. Add it for the myriad nutrients. Blend it and benefit from the extra protein (and no doubt all the other things) and change the bioavailability of the from 25 -95%.

OR if you are not concerned about that, but for a particular smoothie would prefer the texture of the floating chia seeds, similar to an Asian bubble tea, then leave them whole and add it to the final smoothie by just stirring in a couple of table spoons.

Other Things You Can Add At Your Own Wish And Whim To Any Smoothie

- Flaxseed or flax oil: Can impart a strong flavor. High in lignans and omega-3s. The seeds have plenty of fiber.

- Chia. See the section on chia seeds. Add 2-3 tablespoons of chia gel. Store some in the fridge for a ready supply.

- Maca. Not too much for the uninitiated because of its strong taste. I often balance that flavor with tahini. This powder from South America is purported to have benefits for the hormonal and endocrine systems by creating balance.

It's also (among other things) a great source of B12, calcium and magnesium. It is reported to help PMS, menopause symptoms and hot flashes.

- Lucuma is a Peruvian fruit. You probably won't find this delicately flavored tropical fruit in your market. You would use it as a light colored powder which can be described by many as caramel-like, or pumpkin or even slightly malty.

- Spirulina has a strong overpowering taste. Use a <u>tiny</u> bit to start. You can mask any excess taste with apple or celery.

- Wheatgrass. You can add it fresh or even freeze a tray-load by blending it with water and then portioning it out in an ice cube tray. Strongly tasting, I mask it with many things including parsley, mint, celery or apple.

- Apricot kernels. These have vitamin B17 and are purported to have certain anti-cancer qualities. Soaking them will help reduce the toxic cyanogenic glycosides (that bitter almond taste).

- Lemon or lime

- Sweeteners such as dried fruits, agave syrup, rapadura (evaporated and crystallized pure cane sugar juice). Others include honey and maple syrup. I tend to avoid sweetening smoothies unnecessarily.

- Substitute carob for cacao

- Add sprouted chick peas (will create a good consistency). Chick peas (especially raw and sprouted are high in iron and vitamin B but not B12, calcium, zinc, manganese and the list goes on and on)

- Goji or acai berries (you decide if they have more benefits than other berries)

- Mushroom powders (mycelium)

- Apple cider vinegar (with the mother)

- Coconut oil or coconut butter, shredded coconut. I often add the oil or butter to a smoothie

- Nuts, vary your choices to provide different nutrients

- Sesame seeds or tahini, high in calcium

- Bee pollen, has essential amino acids and more

- Probiotics, to boost healthy organisms in the gut

- Antioxidant powders and potions and more ...

The Pragmatic Approach To Sprouts

Sprouts are another contentious issue. I have often heard that there is nothing more nutritious than sprouts, based on their ability to change from a tiny inert seed and potentially transform into a tree. The theory goes, that if a seed can turn into a tree then eating that seed's sprout is definitely going to add a gazillion nutrients to your body.

There are arguments on both sides. It certainly is empowering to believe that eating sprouts is to eat a powerhouse of growth and vitality. It doesn't hurt to believe that sprouts are packed with enzymes, antioxidants, vitamins, minerals, proteins and fiber.

Don't worry, you won't grow a tree inside of you, you're just making sound eating decisions by incorporating some sprouts in your diet.

I have certainly found references that show that the amount of nutrients in sprouts may even be *less* than in the plant. (Another reason to do your own research when you come across various health-claims for particular foods being made!)

Use them in small amounts on occasion anyway, no matter what you believe. Remember to use an array of ingredients available to you.

You may have also heard of 'microgreens' which are really small plants *grown in soil (or soil substitute) that you harvest with the root or seed* (such as you do with sprouts). They are a subset of sprouts.

Common examples are herbs, sunflower sprouts, sorrel or rocket. Restaurants like to use microgreens as attractive garnishes. Just as you will do for your 'macro' greens, you will have to get acquainted with your smaller varieties to be able to work with them. Locate them, taste them, get to know them, use them.

All sprouts including microgreens are best eaten raw and are beautifully suited to blending in smoothies. Some varieties of sprouts are very bland such as alfalfa. Others such as mustard or radish sprouts can have a very strong flavor. Please use the guides in the **Green Smoothie Magic** recipes when choosing your greens.

Remember, you'll find a guide in every recipe as to whether you I recommend mild, strong or a mix of greens to make delicious creations.

As this book is ALL about using easy to find ingredients you'll either find these wonderful greens either in your supermarket, farmers' markets or you can even choose to grow them yourself.

As most of these recipes will have 2 cups of greens indicated in the list, you can either substitute a handful of sprouts or just throw in a few on top of your 'allocation' to pack an even greater nutritious punch.

After all, the more you drink green smoothies, the more you'll enjoy the taste of your greens!

Examples Of Sprouts And Microgreens

The classic sprout you can find almost anywhere is alfalfa. You can also find broccoli sprouts, radish, onion, mustard and chives. They all look pretty much the same! Broccoli and alfalfa are probably the most mild.

Larger varieties are lentil sprouts, mung beans, garbanzo beans (chick peas), sunflower seeds, lentils, buckwheat, soybeans (edamame), quinoa, fenugreek, peas, barley, oats, millet and wheat. These tend to be very easy to distinguish. Mung beans are the 'classic' bean sprouts that you would get in Asian cookery.

Microgreens are pretty much smaller versions of the big plant or mature sprouts! I can find no definitive evidence pointing to them having a better nutritional profile than the large plants. They're simply smaller.

Growing Your Sprouts

You can sprout just about any vegetable or grain: Buckwheat, sesame, lentils, sunflower seeds and grasses.

You can grow your own using no more than seeds, jars, a material such as pantyhose through which water can flow and hold back your sprouts when you're rinsing your babies! I recommend that if you're inclined to grow your own stocks of sprouts, then there are plenty of online resources to show you via video – a quick search on YouTube will get you started!

To start sprouting, you'll need to soak your choice of seed then germinate them. Then you'll have to rinse them several times per day.

If smoothie-making is new to you, then don't take on too much to start. Just buy your sprouts and greens and take things one step at a time.

There are several types of sprouting kits that make it pretty easy to sprout in your kitchen. So get comfortable with your health journey and then take the plunge when you're ready.

You see, you don't *need* to have sprouts to create your concoctions. They are definitely nice to have and a wonderful addition to your repertoire of greens, but you'll find if you just get started with the so-called 'ordinary' ingredients it will be easy to go 'onward and upward' from there.

By the way, one of the big differences between sprouts and microgreens besides plant size is that sprouts that we find in the shops or grow at home are cultivated using water. Microgreens are grown in soil.

Storing Sprouts

Just pop them in the vegetable drawers in your fridge. Microgreens will need to be washed and dried and stored. Sprouts need slightly different treatment. This is important: Use them within 2-3 days. Sometimes you need to rinse sprouts with water especially if you want to prolong their life. The test of their freshness is in the eating. Make sure they're moist fresh and crisp. If they look or feel slimy then just compost them.

Freezing Fruit

In an ideal world you would make smoothies with locally sourced organic produce that is in season. But what if a) the produce is not locally grown, or b) it's not available (for any reason) when you want it? What I would love to suggest to you though is that freezing fruits is a wonderfully useful and delicious thing to do.

You'll do this for a number reasons.

1. Frozen mangoes, bananas, pineapple, peaches, apricots and so on give your smoothies that smooth texture that you're after and that consistency.

2. You can stockpile lots of fruit ready for the months when that fruit is not available fresh for you. At least you'll know where it came from!

3. Berries are fragile and have a short bench or even fridge life. So besides giving great consistency and temperature, berries will last all year round. They give great color to your concoctions too.

4. Frozen fruits are … um … cold! So you may not need to add ice at all.

How To Freeze Fruit For Smoothies

Seems simple. Pop that fruit in the freezer. There is a little more to it however!

Bananas

Peel your bananas. Put them in a container or sealable bag, just one banana deep. They will be much easier to remove. Bananas are not rock hard when frozen. They are actually quite easy to slice from the whole fruit when you have a good knife. Just be careful with all frozen fruit. Keep an eye on your blade and your fingers well away. Try always to apply the blade by securing it in the fruit and then apply the pressure straight down.

I like to keep the bananas whole. When you take the bag or box out of the freezer you'll easily prize the number of bananas you need. All the recipes that need bananas need them in whole units to keep it easy.

You can liberate space in your freezer by placing your already frozen fruit in a resealable bag. Or you can liberate the flatter freezer containers and add more frozen fruit to a deep container that can stay frozen for months without risk of freezer burn to your precious cargo. Just keep whatever you choose well closed.

Pineapple

Peel your pineapple. Cut the pineapple up in wedges that involve a portion of the core. It's best to use sweeter specimens if you can manage. When you cut the fruit, see if the core is particularly woody. You shouldn't have to remove the core. I prefer to blend as much of the usable fruit as possible. The core provides you with great fiber too. If you leave a little of the eyes in the flesh, don't worry too much. It's just a little fiber that will blend up well.

Store in bags and let freeze flat. Then, if you like, you can break up the frozen pieces in the bag. When you need then fruit you'll take out ½ and 1 cup amounts.

Mango

Mango is a sensational fruit in smoothies. Can you tell I love them? I do my very best to store as many mangoes as I can. It's a real delight when I can get the taste of summer in the middle of winter.

There are 2 ways to chop up mangoes. One is to leave the skin on first. Then, with the fruit lengthways take a knife and slice off the cheeks taking the length of the blade to skim it along the broad side of the flat stone. You'll be left with 2 cheeks and the stone, all with flesh on them.

Take a cheek flesh-side up in one palm. Take a tablespoon and introduce the tip between the skin and the flesh and work the tip around the cheek and towards the center. This will pry the flesh away from the skin quite cleanly.

With the stone, remove as much of the flesh as you can and remove the skin too.

Freeze the flesh either in a shallow freezer box or in plastic storage bags. Once frozen for the first time I actually remove the flesh and slice thickly and then replace in the freezer in an airtight container or bag to prevent freezer burn.

You'll find that mango is also quite easy to chop in the frozen state. If you have pieces already roughly chopped then they are simple to portion out with your fingers whenever your recipe calls for it.

Berries

Strawberries, blackberries, blueberries, red and black currants, boysenberries, you name it, they are all excellent candidates for freezing. Berries don't normally stay fresh for long periods of time and some berries have very short availabilities when in season, so freezing makes sense.

Many berries are also available in the freezer section of your supermarket, both organic and non-organic varieties.

However, if you choose to freeze your own here are a couple of tips. Prepare your fruit when you bring them home. Wash them in fresh (possibly filtered) water and then let them drain in a colander and then to dry on a dry tea towel.

Hull your berries if necessary or if called for. Remove any inedible bits. Cut large strawberries into smaller teaspoon size portions while still fresh. Strawberries freeze quite hard and you may find them hard to cut safely.

Freeze flat in a bag or shallow box. They should be as dry as possible when they are put into their containers so that they don't become coated in ice. You can transfer frozen fruit into a deeper container when frozen through.

~ • ~

Green Smoothie 'Rescue' – What To Do If A Recipe Doesn't Work Out!

You know, recipes turn out differently from time to time. When I say add a banana, if you had a banana that's 10 inches long and the time I made it I used a 5 inch banana, well, naturally the output will be a bit different.

Same goes with greens. I have had rocket (or arugula) that is strong and peppery. I have also had it when it's quite mild.

Smoothie recipe results rely on the beauty of nature in all its color and variations. Being a little flexible is sometimes important.

So here are some suggestions for 'rescuing' a not-so-delicious-tasting smoothie.

You'll be pleasantly surprised how often you'll be able to bring one back from the brink of disaster! Rule of thumb? Don't just automatically throw it away if it didn't seem to work.

Too sweet:

- Add more greens. Try some stronger greens. Add herbs such as basil or parsley.

- Parsley is wonderful for reducing sweetness and rebalancing your smoothie without making it bitter.

Too sour or acid:

- Add something to sweeten your recipe. Maybe your apple or pineapple or other fruit was too sour. Raspberries are not very sweet and you may find you need to add something extra. You can add a banana or some mango or grapes or pear to any smoothie to sweeten it up.

- If your smoothie is too sour you can also add more greens – or often what really works is adding some avocado. It has a neutral taste (often) and can soften the sour effect.

- You can also add a sweetener. See below.

Sweeteners you can add:

- Bananas (as mentioned), mango, pear, stevia, agave syrup, honey, rapadura or palm sugar. Basically you want an unprocessed form of sugar.

- A wonderfully nutritious form of sweetener is dried fruit. Try dried peaches, apricots and figs.

Too thick:

- Add water or add ice. Ice can temporarily thicken a smoothie a little because if you add a fair bit it can make your drink a little granita-ish (or in other words similar to a sorbet or slushie).

- The consistency of a smoothie can affect your enjoyment. Add more water if you prefer a thinner smoothie. I prefer thick, Robert prefers thin. We both drink the same smoothies, he just adds more water.

Too gritty:

- Smoothies don't have to be smooth. Sometimes a little something to give it texture creates a different experience for you. I like the variation and will often intentionally add ingredients for the texture.

  You'll find ingredients such as dried figs, cacao nibs, dates (if added at the end to produce a sweet soft chewy speck) can change the mouth feel. Of course I don't think it's gritty then because I like those ingredients. It's all in the mouth of the beholder.

  But perhaps you add the occasional mistake of some husk, or some super fibrousy green that your blender finds difficult to pulverize under normal conditions. It can create a less than optimal experience. Try blending again for another 30 seconds and test.

  If your smoothies are consistently gritty then it could be a matter of needing to either upgrade your blender or put up with it!

Too salty:

- If for some reason your smoothie is too salty, add more greens, some parsley, or more of the dominant flavor in your recipe that you would like to champion. For something neutral add an avocado or more mild greens. Be aware when adding avocado because if your smoothie was designed to be light and fresh and non-creamy it will change the consistency.

Too grassy-tasting:

- If your smoothie tastes a little grassy (and yes, sometimes that happens) add more of the non-green leafy ingredients. A portion of an avocado goes a long way to soothe away many smoothie rescue issues. You can also try a few drops of lemon or lime juice.

Add vanilla:

- When you have a sweeter smoothie that needs a pep-up, vanilla is a wonderful addition. I like to be quite generous with vanilla. You can use essence, powder, paste or even the bean itself.

Add spices:

- Sweet smoothies become even more indulgent with a dash of cinnamon and or nutmeg. Try cloves or cardamom (they definitely make a lovely chai-tasting smoothie). They complement vanilla beautifully. Cinnamon also adds something special to non-sweet smoothies too.

- Experiment with a sprinkle of cumin or a curry powder. Cayenne is one of those superfoods that has many health benefits from digestive to circulatory stimulation and more. You can add a dash of cayenne to a sweet OR a savory smoothie.

Add lemon:

- When your smoothie needs to cut back on sweetness try adding ½ teaspoon of lemon. Watch out because it's easy to go too gung ho on the lemon. A few drops may be all you need.

Add salt:

- Remember to only use sea salt for ANY food, ever. Don't touch that table salt. It's really not good for you at all. Believe it or not, salt can really bring out the sweetness in your food. If you're making a sweet smoothie grind a few grains of salt into the mix and you'll be in for a pleasant surprise. Think of adding salt to a drink that needs a flavor boost. You could add Bragg Liquid Aminos too.

Add ginger:

- Ginger is great for adding a little zing. If you add a very small amount you will find it lifts your smoothie. The more you add the spicier it tastes. Ginger has great benefit to the immune system, helps with motion sickness, pain relief and inflammation amongst other things.

About Blenders And Blending

The Best Blenders For Smoothies

The better your blender the better the blend! Sounds like a no-brainer really. Do a little research. I know you can find a good blender at many price points.

When I say a good blender the only thing that matters is the result you get. Generally the better blenders are more powerful (upwards of 1000 watts). They may or may not have programs for smoothies or other foods that you will make.

Most importantly you want them to give you the possibility of a smooth blend. My old blender did an OK job. My less expensive new one is brilliant. Read the reviews on Amazon as a good starting point. Look for those that have consistent 4 and 5 star reviews. If they have lots with 1 and 2 stars then see if there are any recurring issues and if you would live with them. For example, you may be fine putting up with a glass jug if that's a reason for a low review.

The very popular brands that are most recommended for blending are Vitamix and Blendtec. These tend to be more expensive. There are very well reviewed alternative choices that sell for under $60 (US dollars). For a mid-range and probably better choice of options and power you can pay up to $120.

Other brands are Hamilton Beach, Froothie, Mixtec, Omega, Magic Bullet, Oster and Sunbeam. There are plenty more.

Generally a lower price blender will not stand the test of time. So be aware that buying a cheaper blender may mean you have to replace it or upgrade sooner. I know people who have top of the range blenders (such as Vitamix and Blendtec) that have lasted many, many years.

Can you use the blender that comes with your food processor?

Yes you can, however I have found that the best blenders are those purpose-built. If that's what you've got now, then start with that and upgrade. I don't advise buying a food processor and attached blender.

Can you use a food processor instead of a blender?

That does not work well. The blend will not be smooth and while it could work as a stop gap, you'll find many food processors neither have the jug shape nor the power or the blade configuration to cope with the vigors of blending.

Choosing Your Blender

Here Are The Best Things To Look For In A Blender:

- **Over 1000 watts of power if you can afford it**. Your blend is likely to be less smooth if you buy blenders of lower power. More powerful blenders will easily crush ice and pulverize berries.

- I prefer a **BPA-free polycarbonate (plastic) jug**. Pay particular attention to the blender specifications to check the quality of the plastic. Check for dishwasher safety. You will have to remove the blades if you want to put the jug in the dishwasher.

  Because of the secure and stable way most plastic jugs fits over the motor you may find it easy to keep the part of the coupling that fits into the motor unit (that sits on the bench) completely dry. This may prolong the life of your unit. With my blender I can easily clean the jug with water, mild detergent and still keep the bottom of the jug out of water.

  Plastic jugs may not stay crystal clear forever. They are not entirely resistant to scratches. Small price to pay if you have everything else you need.

- **Glass jugs** are heavy even when empty. They can be prone to breakage. You don't want to be stuck with a glass pitcher that shatters. Read all reviews to see what people complain about. Once you remove the blades you can easily clean a glass jug in the dishwasher.

  The thing I really disliked about my glass jar blender was having to use the sealing ring between the jar and the blade unit. The seal progressively failed over time and this created mess. I prefer the way the plastic jugs are molded and the unit fits over positioners on the base and there is no fiddling around. The seal is evident.

- If you look for a machine with a **wide stable metal base** then it will be more sturdy.

- A **blender with a tamper** that fits into the lid is ideal. A tamper will allow you to guide food onto the blades while the blender is in operation without risk of damage to the unit or the tamper. It also creates a seal that will largely stop any food from being expelled out of the top during use.

- Choose a blender that's **easy to clean**. Touch pads are far easier to clean because of their smoother profile than their cousins; push buttons. Clean up spillages or drips as soon as you can and you will be able to keep most blenders clean.

- The better blenders will have **one-touch operation** for different programs. You will find smoothie, ice crushing, cleaning programs among others. It's nice to have infinite speed dials in addition to preset programs.

Various Blenders And Price Indications

Here are just a handful of suggestions listing the inexpensive brands first. I recommend researching them online (best place to start is Amazon!). Look at the features and the reviews (handy to check on the issues and customers experiences).

- <u>Hamilton Beach</u> has a personal single serve blender from about $20 up to low to mid-priced blenders

- <u>Oster Fusion Blender</u> (only 600 watts of power)

- <u>Oster Beehive Blender</u> (600W) from around $55

- <u>Magic Bullet</u> (a personal use small capacity blender with great reviews) around $50, but you do need to trim things down a lot to fit ingredients in.

- <u>Kitchen Aid Blenders</u> start from $99.

- <u>JTC Omniblend</u> has models starting at $250 (3 HP motor, the information says it is more powerful than both Vitamix and Blendtec). This looks like a great place to start.

- <u>Blendtec</u>: Many models ranging from about $370

- <u>Vitamix</u>: Many models ranging from around $450 to high end prices

I actually live in Australia and brands like Vitamix are much more expensive than in the US and therefore prohibitively expensive for many. I decided to test drive a lower priced blender for the purposes of reviewing a different model. I spent only $200 on a fantastic Sunbeam blender (Café Series, PB9800) with 2000W of power and a 2 liter jug. So I am very happy.

Blending Techniques

So, you have your blender and it's time to use it. For the most part you can put your ingredients into your blender and press the go button! Some blenders have a smoothie program which you can deploy and your smoothie is done. For a smoother result you may even choose to put it through that program more than one time.

For the sake of this discussion, my blender's smoothie program is only 23 seconds and works very well even on one press.

The more powerful or higher quality your blender the less blending steps. In my old blender I would first have had to blend the harder or more fibrous components with some water. If nuts were in the recipe I would certainly have had quite obvious yet small chunks of nuts. The blend was inconsistent.

This is why if I suggest nuts or seeds in one of the *Green Smoothie Magic* recipes, and if your blender is perhaps not as powerful or effective as you like, you should blend those nuts or seeds first with water to make a milk. Then, without straining the pulp out you add your other ingredients and blend again.

However, if you have a good blender you may only need to pop everything into the jug at one time, put the lid on and press the go button!

What Do I Do If The Blend Is Not Smooth Enough?

If your smoothie doesn't look or feel smooth enough then re-blend. Sometimes you will crave or enjoy a smoothie that is *not* completely smooth. You can pulverize your ingredients without blending them into a creamy consistency if you wish. Remember you can add dates, cacao nibs, dried figs, apricots or raisins right at the end (instead of along with the other ingredients). It's really enjoyable to have a tiny speck of texture that provides a different consistency and flavor burst. See what you enjoy.

About Drinking And Storing Your Smoothie

How Long Can You Keep Them?

If your smoothie is kept cool you can keep them all day. Maybe you can take your smoothie to work (or school or wherever you're going) in a mason or other jar.

The taste of a smoothie may change over time. Usually they are very good throughout the day. I have experimented with keeping aside smoothies to try the next day and some are great and others have lost that certain 'something'.

Consume your smoothie the same day you make it. They should be kept covered (in an airtight container if possible) to reduce the amount of oxidation of the ingredients.

How Long To Drink It (Gulp It Down?)

Smoothies are wonderful to linger over. Rather than gulping them down you can really enjoy every mouthful. Take your time. These potions can last you for a few hours if you like. Some people put them in a jar and take them to work to either have as a meal or to sip on throughout the morning.

We have really been conditioned to eat too quickly. Take this chance to slow it down (if you have that luxury).

Some smoothies I have made with stronger greens such as mustard leaves tend to develop a stronger taste the longer the smoothie sits. It is great if you like a spicy smoothie. Just be warned because it could take you by surprise if you enjoy taking your time drinking your smoothies!

Drinking Your Smoothie Cold – Is Too Cold Bad?

What temperature you ask! Well, you have to find a happy medium between too warm and too cold and icy. How you like a smoothie will also depend on the type that you are making and the weather.

For the most part, I personally don't like my smoothies too cold unless it's summer. An icy smoothie will appear less sweet and it will appear to have less flavor.

Smoothies that are too warm CAN be a little cloying or icky (for want of a better word). It will always depend on what you put in them. For example a salad type of smoothie that has little sweetness, is definitely better taken 'cool to cold'. Maybe you will have more tolerance for a warmish dessert style or pudding type smoothie.

All the recipes use 1 cup of water to start. Follow the directions and then make your final adjustments with water and ice. If you're unsure taste your smoothie out of the jug with a spoon. In doing so you'll sample its consistency and its temperature. You'll know whether you need or want to add ice or more water and in what quantity.

The Best Way To Drink Your Smoothies

You can drink, spoon or sip a smoothie. Use a spoon or a straw or simply pick up your glass and enjoy it. Drink it slowly enough for your enzymes to start working in the mouth and to avoid indigestion. These blends are sustainable energy in a glass. They will fill you up in a satisfying way. Just like anything you should never eat or drink too fast.

Time To Get Started!

It's time to start making smoothies. Here are well over 132 recipes for you to try! Remember you WILL have favorites. Come and tell me which ones.

Green Smoothie Magic 101: Instructions At A Glance For Blending Any Smoothie

Blending your smoothie is something you're going to do with every recipe. So naturally I am giving you those instructions here so that you don't need to read the same instructions on every page.

Put your ingredients into the blender.
Blend until your smoothie has the consistency that you like.

That all seems simple enough! I actually have a one-touch 'smoothie program' on my blender and because it's quite a short program, sometimes I have to put it on a second time in order to incorporate everything well.

There will be times when you want your smoothie ultra-smooth and other times where you like a little something to chew or feel under the tooth. A change inconsistency will happen with the different recipes.

How Much Will Each Recipe Make?

Each recipe in this book makes, in general, somewhere between 1 ½ to 2 ½ big glasses of green smoothie. Rather than try to get the same volume out of every recipe, my aim is to give you recipes that have a good balance between the 2 cups minimum of greens in every smoothie and the other ingredients.

Reminder 1: What Greens To Use?

Remember you can do a 'greens exchange' on most smoothies. When your recipe says to pop in 2 cups of mild greens, consult your fridge (!) and your mild greens list.

There will be times you get a specific recommendation. That's more likely to be when you add a strong green (see the list) as there is more of a difference in result between watercress and mustard leaves (both strong) than there is between using say, cabbage, chickweed, spinach or mizuna lettuce.

Reminder 2: Adding Water And Ice

Each recipe will have at least 1 cup of fluid in it. It will be either water, coconut water or nut/seed milk (or nuts/seed and water).

How much ice you add and how much extra water you add to your smoothie will depend on your personal preference for temperature and consistency.

The temperature of your smoothie will also be dependent on whether you put frozen or fresh fruit in. The more frozen fruit in will probably mean less ice added.

Just know that if you are new to making green smoothies that you will have fun experimenting with getting the balance right for you. Smoothie making is not an exact science (because of the variables of natural produce) and it really is hard to make mistakes. This also means that each time a particular recipe may taste a tiny bit different to you.

Sometimes you can be a bit generous with a green or say with lemon juice. Whatever it is, check out Green Smoothie Rescue notes in the introduction if you need to 'fix' anything.

Reminder 3: Nuts And Nut Milk

If you have nut milk at home then feel free to use it. In my recipes I have opted for a simple approach that gives you the nutrition of the whole nut.

For best results you will soak the nuts or seeds to get rid of any enzyme inhibitors, to soften the nuts for better blending, and if present reduce any amount of glycosides that could be present.

If you don't have time to soak then that's OK. They will still blend well. Realize that even a short soak time is better than no soak time. Sunflower seeds for example need only 20-30 minutes while almonds are better soaked overnight. Know that you can still get some benefit from short soak.

You'll get in the habit of having an amount of soaked nuts on hands. So here's what to do ...

Place the amount of soaked nuts or seeds indicated in the recipe into the blender along with 1 cup of water.

Blend until smooth. This will vary depending on the blender that you use.

No need to strain. This is a simple one-step way of including nuts without fuss.

Remember you can always simply use water or coconut water instead, or even commercial nut (or any other variety such as quinoa, millet, rice) milks.

Reminder 4: Adding Sweeteners

You'll find some smoothies that recommend adding a little sweetness for balance (if it is not coming from the fruit components alone).

If you are adding for nutritional value then arguably you would firstly consider adding one of dried peaches, dried apricots, dried figs and raisins.

After that you would consider adding agave syrup, dates, honey and then lastly stevia. Unfortunately commercially available stevia can be quite processed and the natural herb can take some getting used to. Choose wisely.

You can add dried fruit by just chopping them up. Or you can soak them first to soften them. It really depends on how good your blender is and if you like to feel little specks in your smoothie or always like a silky smooth drink. If you do soak your fruit, cover the fruit with water. You can keep soaked fruit in the fridge. Use the soak water.

Reminder 5: Adding In Superfoods

If you have a stock of superfoods (those listed in the previous pages) then feel free to add them in. This book is filled with recipes that when thoughtfully made with good wholesome ingredients will give you excellent nutritional balance and are packed with nature's ordinary superfoods.

There are plenty of inexpensive everyday items on that superfoods list (such as almonds, coconut oil, spirulina so you don't need to go crazy buying the latest touted hyper-marketed product (unless you want to).

Reminder 6: Scoring smoothies

You'll find on a few dozen smoothies I have given them a score. I don't do it for all of them. I just do it because there are some instances where it's worth knowing what others have thought of something. Don't get hung up on what others thought.

However, I did learn one thing from this whole experience. It's better to let any unsuspecting subject know what's in their smoothie so they can anticipate it.

You see, when you go to a restaurant, you order according to your tastes and you know what's coming. Robert (my hubby) finds it easier to score them when he can – in a way – pretend he ordered them from his favorite café.

Reminder 7: Have Fun And Enjoy Your Smoothie Adventures

Putting these smoothies together is different to adding ingredients into a pot for cooking. You'll find many that tempt you because they have your favorite ingredients. You'll also find some recipe combinations that may not even seem to work well together when you read them.

How adventurous you are is up to you. So, take a lesson from my 9 year old. As I have said before, giving anything to my daughter like a bowl of chopped cabbage, fennel and pineapple would simply NEVER work. But those ingredients in a smoothie worked for her and she lapped up every last drop.

Now it's your turn ...

Recipe Index Cross-Referenced For Major Ingredient

In the following section you'll find ALL the recipes 1-132 in no particular order. I pondered this and discussed it endlessly - "should we 'categorize' the recipes etc?" - in the end we decided that the best method is to be constantly inspired and surprised by reading through and not to fall into choosing something you "think" you will like just because it falls into a "category".

But this can make it harder to see your chosen ingredient in a list of recipes ... so ... we made a "*Recipe Index*" which cross-references lists of recipes by major ingredient - think of it as a sub-table of contents.

So as not to complicate the book for new readers AND to keep the information and main Table of Contents clear, these are located at the back of the book.

Green Smoothie Magic Recipes

1.   Classic Pine-Mint Smoothie

This recipe is indeed a classic. Simple and reliably delicious and good for a newbie to green smoothies. Two cups is a lot of pineapple so it's best to use a sweet(ish) one. If it's too acid or sour then add more leaves and some sweetener. You could add dried figs or apricots or soft dates. See notes on the pages just before the recipes.

> 1 cup water
> 2 cups pineapple (fresh or frozen)
> 1 avocado
> 1 cup mint leaves
> 1 cup of spinach leaves or other mild green

Ice and extra water to get to your desired temperature and consistency.

2.   Cinnamango Smoothie

I love this smoothie. Then again, I love just about any smoothie with mango in it. I freeze as much fresh mango as I can in summer to enjoy this anytime through the year. This smoothie regularly scores 9 and 10.

If you have a very efficient blender just add everything in at the one time. Otherwise blend your smoothie in 2 stages making your nut milk first and then adding the other ingredients.

In place of the water and almonds, you can use prepared almond milk, plain filtered water or even coconut water.

Blend first

> 1 cup water
> ¼ cup almonds (soaked for about 6 hrs min if possible)

Then add

> 1 cup mango (frozen)
> Cinnamon, salt and vanilla
> 2 cup spinach leaves (or any combination of mild greens)
> 1 tbsp chopped mint leaves

Ice and extra water to get your desired temperature and consistency

3.   Mangolicious Strawberry-Mint

Another simply delicious green smoothie that always scores very highly.

> 1 cup rice or almond milk (use commercial variety, your own pre-prepared milk or first blend ¼ cup almonds and 1 cup of water)
> ½ cup chopped mint leaves or more!
> 1.5 cups sweet potato leaves (or any mild greens)
> ½ cup mango (frozen)
> ½ cup strawberry (frozen)
> Pinch sea salt
> Cinnamon to taste (optional)

Add water or ice as desired

4. Bananaberry Cream

This smoothie calls for some yogurt (preferably non-dairy). If you don't have any yogurt and still want it to be creamier than it would be with those 2 bananas then add ½ an avocado. My 9 year old scores this 9 out of 10!

2 bananas
½ cup soy yogurt or coconut yogurt
2 cups of baby spinach leaves (or any combination of mild greens)
1 cup berries (I use frozen raspberries or mixed berries)
Pinch of sea salt
1 cup water

Ice (for texture and temperature)

5. Mango Delight

I love this very refreshing and vitalizing smoothie. The quality and strength of lime juice can vary, so I recommend starting with 1 tablespoon of juice first and then adding more after.

While this one is VERY much to my taste (hitting a high 9.5) it scored a highly respectable 8 out of 10 chez moi! See what you think!

½ cup water
1-2 tbsp lime juice (start with 1 tbsp and add to taste)
1.5 cups of cos/romaine lettuce (or any combination of mild greens)
¼ cup parsley
¼ cup of mint
1 apple, chopped (no stalk but leave everything else including the seeds)
1 cup of mango (I use frozen)

Water and ice to get the right consistency and temperature

6. Vanilla Chai Smoothie

My daughter gave the name to this delicious smoothie. She scores this one 9.5 out of 10. It's smooth, sweet and dessert-like with a hint of spice. A real winner.

In this recipe I use a handful of seeds and nuts for texture and great nutritional benefit. Handfuls vary from hand to hand, so as a rule add no more than a ¼ cup. Soak them if you have a chance. A short time is better than no time at all.

I also use dried figs and apricots. They give texture as well as a caramel-like natural sweetness. You could use agave or stevia but you would miss out on the nutrient profile of these little beauties. In this recipe I use 3 of each because besides a natural sweetness (especially with non-sulfured organic fruit which taste a little more caramelized) they have lots of calcium along with many other nutrients. So ...

First blend

> 1 cup water
> 1 handful of sunflower seeds
> 1 handful of almonds

Then add

> 2 tbsp chia gel (presoaked chia seeds)
> 6 dried fruit chopped (figs and apricots)
> ½ avocado
> 2 cups of mild greens in any combination. (Try spinach, mizuna or chickweed, sweet potato leaves or any from your mild greens list)
> ½ tsp of cinnamon
> ¼ tsp of nutmeg
> 1-2 tsps of vanilla
> A pinch of clove or cardamom is optional
> Dash of sea salt
> 1 cup of ice

Add water and ice for your desired consistency and temperature.

7.   Choc-Chai Smoothie

Use dried fruit for sweetness and a little texture under the tooth! Your final step in this smoothie after blending your Vanilla Chai Smoothie is to add and then blend your ¼ cup of cacao nibs.

Why nibs instead of powder? Well because after much experimentation I have decided that you get a better result with nibs. Powder gives a bitter more pervasive flavor which for me changes the whole flavor profile by masking the other tastes. With nibs you taste all the different flavors in a complementary fashion! I really like this one.

Do you prefer to add cacao powder? Then start with 1 teaspoon and add. I know people who say the more cacao powder the better. It really is VERY personal.

First blend

    1 cup water
    1 handful of sunflower seeds
    1 handful of almonds

Then add

    2 tbsp chia gel
    6 dried fruit chopped
    ½ avocado
    2 cups of mild greens
    ½ tsp of cinnamon, ¼ tsp of nutmeg, 1-2 tsps of vanilla, optional clove or cardamom powder, dash of sea salt

Then as a final step

    Add 1 cup of ice and
    ¼ cup of cacao nibs. Blend so that they are broken down for texture and a burst of flavor in every mouthful.

8.   Banana-Choc-Chai Smoothie

You guessed it. This is another variation on a theme. If you like the Chai series of recipes then you will find that each one although very similar gives a totally different result. And I mean totally.

First blend

　1 cup water
　1 handful of sunflower seeds
　1 handful of almonds

Then add

　1 frozen banana
　2 tbsp chia gel
　6 dried fruit chopped (figs and or apricots)
　½ avocado
　2 cups of mild greens in any combination. Use spinach, mizuna, chickweed, sweet potato leaves or others from your mild greens list
　½ tsp of cinnamon, ¼ tsp of nutmeg, 1-2 tsps of vanilla, Dash of sea salt

Then as a final step add

　¼ cup of cacao nibs
　1 cup of ice

9. Banana Raspberry Yum

This is another perennial favorite. Just about everyone I make this for gives it a minimum 9 out of 10 score. I am sure it will be for you too. Remember that if you are using any frozen fruit then you'll probably need more water and less ice. Fresh fruit usually means you start with 1 cup of water to blend and then add ice to get that pleasing coolness that a smoothie seems to need! You can throw in a handful of almonds with a cup of milk if you don't have almond milk. When in doubt or if there are not nuts in the cupboard, use water. It will still be delicious.

> 1 cup almond milk (or other nut milk, or add ¼ cup almonds and blend with water first))
> 1.5 cups raspberries (frozen)
> 2 bananas (fresh or frozen)
> 1 cup spinach
> 1 cup romaine (cos) lettuce (or 2 cups total mild greens of any combination)
> ¼ cup chopped mint leaves

Ice

10.   Berrylicious

This is a wonderful smoothie for the uninitiated and a simply great place to start for children. It has tons of berries and banana.

> 1 cup water
> 1 cup raspberries (fresh or frozen)
> 1 cup other berries (fresh or frozen)
> 2 bananas
> 2 cups spinach (or mild greens in any combination)
> Sea salt, cinnamon and vanilla

Add ice and water for desired thickness and temperature

11.   Pineapple Broccoli Sensation

You know, I still think it's surprising I can cram as much raw broccoli as I do into a smoothie and get great results. Blended with the right ingredients you can determine whether it's a taste to complement or one to be masked without anyone being the wiser. The broccoli in this smoothie enhances the other greens and helps reduce the acidity of the pineapple. It consistently scores a 9. Sweeter pineapples are always better in smoothies by the way.

> 1 cup water
> 1 medium tomato, chopped
> 2 cups mild greens (try romaine/cos or baby spinach)
> ½ cup broccoli florets
> 1 cup pineapple (no skin)
> ¼-1/3 cup cilantro (coriander) leaves and stems

Ice

12.   Pineapple Dilly Dally

What can I say? My girl loves this very green delicious smoothie. She scored it 9.75. Oh, happy me.

You can use lemon juice instead of lime if you wish. It's optional to use ½ an avocado to 'smooth it up' even more.

    1 cup water
    ¼ cup dill
    1 tbsp lime juice
    1 tomato
    1 cup kale
    1 cup bok or pak choy (don't feel constrained. If you don't have kale and choy, just use 2 cups mild greens. Remember to vary your green intake)
    1.5 cups pineapple
    OPTIONAL: ½ avocado

Add ice and water for desired temperature and consistency

13.   Herbal Ginger Beet

Even though I have a good blender, I do like to blend the carrot and beet first with water to get a smoother consistency of the final product. You can use any proportion of the 2 cups of greens as mild and strong. Taste test your leaves. Mustard can be VERY strong especially if you sip your smoothie over time. The spiciness seems to develop. The safer 'strong' greens to start with are usually watercress and rocket. Be brave, you're going to find there are a lot of these recipes that taste surprisingly fantastic with strong greens.

First blend

I cup water
¼ cup beet chopped
¼ cup carrot chopped small
Small amount ginger

Then add

1 cup mild greens (for eg: spinach, kale, choy, sweet potato leaves)
1 cup strong greens (rocket, watercress or mustard leaves)
¼ cup cilantro/coriander
½ cup broccoli
1 cup water

Finally

1 cup ice and blend again

Recommendations

To add taste bud drama, add cayenne and lime juice.
Vary the amount of strong greens to your taste. Prefer mild greens? Then use 2 cups.

14.   Saladicious

This one's packed with many great ingredients, almost like a liquid salad. The sweetness is mild and comes from the beet and carrot. The basic smoothie is really quite mild. Because it's more green and less sweet it seems to be better for green smoothie aficionados. The parsley, ginger and lime lift it. For more taste bud action add in some cayenne and cumin.

First blend

> 1 cup water
> ¼ cup beet chopped
> ¼ cup carrot chopped small
> Small amount ginger

Then add

> ½ avocado
> 1 cup mild greens (spinach, kale, choy, sweet potato leaves)
> 1 cup strong greens (rocket, watercress or mustard leaves)
> ¼ cup cilantro/coriander
> 1 cup parsley
> Sea salt
> 2 tbsp lime juice

1 cup ice and blend again

Recommendations

> To green it up even more add a stalk of celery or a cup of broccoli
> Add some cayenne pepper and cumin

15.   Salad Sunset

Sweet and savory in one. The pineapple really does a good job to complement the vegetables here.

First blend

   1 cup water
   ¼ cup beet chopped
   ¼ cup carrot chopped small
   Small amount ginger

Then add

   1 cup pineapple
   ½ avocado
   2 cups greens (incorporating mild and up to 1 cup strong greens)
   ¼ cup cilantro/coriander
   ¼ cup broccoli

Ice

16. Blue Bat

Blueberries always impart a great dark color to any smoothie. You can treat this one as a base to make other recommended smoothie variations below.

    1 cup water
    1 cup blueberries (frozen or fresh)
    2 cups mild greens (try a choy, mizuna, cabbage)
    1 kiwi fruit (with hard end removed)
    1 small tomato

Ice and then blend

Recommendations

For extra sweetness add some apple, ½ cup pineapple or a date or 2
To create different taste sensations: Add mint OR coriander/cilantro

17.   Blueberry Pineapple Smoothie

My darling girl scored this one 8.5!

The complement of greens in this smoothie is made up of celery, cilantro and the mild green of your choice.

1 cup pineapple
2 tomatoes
1 cup blueberries (frozen or fresh)
¼ cup coriander
1 cup spinach leaves or other mild leafy green
1 stick celery chopped
1 squeeze of lemon to taste

Ice as required

18.   Berry Packed Smoothie

The tang of raspberries, the color of blueberries and the sweetness of bananas.

Blend first

1 cup water
¼ cup (soaked) almonds

Then add

1 cup raspberries
¼ cup blueberries
1 banana
½ cup broccoli
1 small-medium tomato
1.5 cup spinach leaves

Ice

19.   What A Lovely Pear

In this smoothie I have recommended using kale. The rest of your 2 cup greens component is mint. When I use any green I will use as much of the stalk as I can. Just get rid of the woody ends. I don't think it's good policy to just use the leaves as you'll miss out on a lot of nutrition and fiber. It's all (in this case) good!

1 cup water
1 pear
1 orange peeled
1 cup pineapple
½ cup mint
1.5 cup kale (or other mild green)

Ice as required

20. Tangy Tex Mex

The smoothness of avocado balanced with sweet, salty and tangy flavors with a touch of cilantro.

1 cup water
½ cup pineapple
½ large avocado
2 tomatoes
½ cup red bell pepper
1.5 cups greens (your choice, mild or strong)
½ cup cucumber
¼ cup coriander
1 tbsp lime juice (add more to increase the tang)
Pinch cayenne pepper (to taste)
Pinch sea salt

Ice

21. Dance To The Beet

Orange provides some of the liquid so I only added ½ cup water to start.

½ cup water
1 orange
¼ cup beet
¼ - ½ cup parsley
2 cups greens according to preference. I use 1 cup mild (spinach, asparagus lettuce or chickweed) and 1 cup strong (watercress or rocket)
Ginger

1 cup ice

22. Mango Spice

Your kids will give this the thumbs up!

Blend first

> 1 cup water
> 8 brazil nuts (or use a cup of nut milk or plain water)

Then add

> ½ avocado
> 2 cups mild greens (such as tatsoi or chickweed)
> 1 cup mango (frozen or fresh)
> 1 tsp cinnamon, ½ tsp nutmeg
> Vanilla

> 1 cup ice

Recommendations

> If you need more sweetness, add more mango or 2 pieces of dried fruit. I like the feel under the tooth. You could sweeten with agave syrup or stevia although I tend towards fruit if I can help it.
> Clove or cardamom powder can deepen the spice profile for you

23. Choc-Mango Spice

Gets the green light!

Blend first

1 cup water
8 brazil nuts
(or use a cup of nut milk)

Then add

2 cups mild greens (in any combination)
1 cup frozen mango
½ avocado
Vanilla
1 tsp cinnamon, ½ tsp nutmeg
¼ cup cacao nibs (or some cacao powder to taste)
1 cup ice

Recommendations

If you need more sweetness, add ½ cup more mango or 2 pieces of dried fruit. Clove or cardamom powder are other handy spices that complement cinnamon and nutmeg.

24. Blue Eyes Smoothie

If you're lucky enough to have fresh blueberries on hand you may want to throw in ½ cup of ice to the blend. Right up there with goodness, taste and score to boot.

    1 cup water
    1 cup blueberries (frozen or fresh)
    1 apple
    ½ cup coriander
    1 stalk celery
    1.5 cups mild greens
    Sea salt
    Lemon juice to taste

Ice as you need it!

Recommendation

To create a different experience add in a handful of mint

25.　Vanilla Pudding Smoothie

This smoothie (which unbelievably almost always scores 10 out of 10) is packed with nutritious brazil nuts, avocado and of course a mountain of leafy greens. It will be THICK so to make it drinkable, add more water ½ cup at a time. Actually I like to eat this one with a spoon, like a pudding dessert.

First blend the nuts and water. Then add in the other ingredients.

½ cup brazil nuts
1 cup water
2 dates (remove the pits of course ;))
½ avocado
1.5 – 2 tsp vanilla
¼ tsp sea salt
2 cups mild greens (use spinach or chickweed)

Ice if you need it

Recommendation

Instead of dates add dried peaches or apricots for even more nutrition. Soak them (adding soak water too) if you want them very smooth.

26.   Carob Vanilla Spice Pudding Smoothie

OK, OK, so it looks very similar to *Vanilla Pudding*, but that's just on paper. But it is different and it is SO good you need to know how to make this one in its own right.

Blend first

> 1 cup water
> ½ cup cashews (soaked if you have them available, dry will do)
> 3 dates (no stone. Or other dried fruit)

Then add

> 2 tbsp carob
> 1 small avocado, or ½ large
> 2 cups mild greens
> ¼ - ½ tsp cinnamon
> Vanilla
> Pinch sea salt

1 cup ice or as needed

Recommendation

Instead of dates add dried peaches or apricots for even more nutrition. Soak them (adding soak water too) if you want them very smooth.

27.   Mint Vanilla Pudding Smoothie

If you want to drink this delicious smoothie, keep adding water until you get your desired consistency. It's beautifully suited to using a spoon and savoring every last mouthful.

First blend the nuts and water. Then add in the other ingredients.

½ cup brazil nuts
1 cup water
2 dates
½ avocado
1.5 – 2 tsp vanilla
¼ tsp salt
1 cup mild greens (use spinach or chickweed)
1 cup mint

Ice, if you will!

Recommendation

Instead of dates add dried peaches or apricots for even more nutrition. Soak them (adding soak water too) if you want them very smooth.

28. Kiwi Vanilla Smoothie

What can I say? This cornucopia of interesting ingredients turns out a delicious 10/10 scoring smoothie!

If you don't have sprouts on hand just add an extra ½ cup of mild greens.

First blend:

Handful of almonds
1 cup water

Then add

2 dates
1 tsp vanilla essence
2 kiwi
¼ tsp salt
1 cup kale (or mild greens)
½ cup broccoli
Handful of sprouts

Recommendation

Substitute your dates with dried peaches or apricots for even more nutrition. Soak them (adding soak water too) if you want them very smooth.

29.   Freshly Minted

Remember if you don't want to use nut milk or almonds just use water or even coconut water. The mint transforms this into another high scoring and different smoothie. Enjoy it!

First blend:

Handful of almonds
1 cup water

Then add:

2 kiwi
¼ cup broccoli
2 dates
1 cup kale
1 cup mint
Handful of sprouts
1 tsp vanilla essence
¼ tsp salt

Recommendation

Dried peaches or apricots can be used instead of dates for even more nutrition. Soak them (adding soak water too) if you want them very smooth.

30. Iron Maiden Smoothie

Delight in this not so green looking smoothie that packs an iron punch! So good that my 9 year old rates this one 12/10!

½ cup raspberries
½ cup strawberries
2 bananas
1.5 cup sweet potato leaves (or other mild greens)
¼ -½ cup parsley
1 cup water

Ice

31. Mint Magic

This mild-flavored smoothie is great with generous helpings of vanilla, spice and mint. Feel free to add extra mint.

The chia gel (if it's been presoaked in water) ups the ante on the protein amount. You'll get way more into your system if you blend the chia with the smoothie. Unblended chia gel really gives a great 'bubble tea' texture that's interesting. Actually it's quite alluring for children!

1 cup water
½ large avocado
4 dates
Vanilla 1 tsp essence or ½ tsp powder (or more to taste)
½ tsp cinnamon
½ tsp nutmeg
A pinch of clove or cardamom powder if you are partial to it
1.5 cups greens of your choice (mild greens)
½ cup mint leaves
2 tbsp chia gel (either blend or stir in after for the texture of a bubble tea)

Ice

Recommendation

Dried peaches or apricots or raisins can be used instead of dates. They are more nutritious. Soak them (adding soak water too) if you want them very smooth.

32.   Stevie's Punch

My friend Steve loved and named this one! I bet you guessed that little fact. You can trust that if Steve wanted to name it that it scored top marks!

1 apple
1 cup pineapple
1.5 cup nut milk (I used a small handful each of macadamia and walnut added to 1 cup of water)
¼ cup cilantro/coriander
2 cups mild greens

Ice

33.   Kiwi Dill Elixir

Blend this simply tasty high-scoring smoothie and marvel how dill and kiwi are such great partners.

If your blender is not powerful enough then you may want to chop the little hard bit off the stalk end of your kiwi. I never peel my kiwi for a smoothie because it adds fiber.

    1 cup water
    2 cups of mild greens (try bok choy, mizuna, chickweed)
    1 stalk celery
    ¼ cup dill
    2 kiwi

Ice

34.   Strawberry Kiwi Sunshine

This variation on a kiwi dill theme is completely different with the addition of strawberries.

    1 cup water
    1 cup strawberries (frozen or fresh)
    2 kiwi
    2 cups of mild greens (try bok choy, spinach, chickweed)
    1 stalk celery
    ¼ cup dill

Ice, blend and drink your green smoothie

35.   Minted Pear Smoothie

As usual there are 2 cups of salad leaves in this recipe! The strength of the cress or other strong leaves really lends this smoothie a pleasing bite. Feel free to change the proportions of the strong leaves to taste.

    1 cup water
    ½ cup broccoli
    1 pear
    ¼ - ½ cup mint
    1 cup mild leaves such as baby spinach
    1 cup strong leaves such as watercress

Ice and water in just the right amounts!

36. Lime Ginger Dill Smoothie

My husband Robert really likes this one. What a great lime color! Yeah baby!

1 pear
½ cucumber (or 1 cup)
¼ cup dill
1 sm-med avocado or half a large
1 cup mild greens (sweet potato or kale)
1 stalk celery
1-3 tbsp lime juice, start with 1 tbsp and work upwards to taste
Ginger, to taste

Ice

37. Poppy Celebration Smoothie

This one has all the fruit that my Dad would love if he were with us. It's a kind of memorial smoothie in my house. You'll need ice if all your fruit is fresh and not frozen.

½ cup mango
½ cup guava (I use frozen guava pulp)
½ cup pineapple
½ cup raspberries
½ cup blueberries
1.5 cups Coconut water
Sea salt
2 pieces of dried fruit (apricot, peach or some raisins, soaked if you like)
2 cups mild greens
½ cup cilantro/coriander

Ice

38. Fennel Refresher

Lots of green stuff, tons of flavor. Fennel definitely makes this a taste sensation. The salt gives it a flavor boost. Try it.

1 stalk celery
1 pear
½ cup fennel
1 cup parsley
1 cup greens of your choice
1-2 tbsp lemon optional
1 cup water
Pinch sea salt

Add ½ cup ice or more and blend away

39. Apricana Smoothie

These humble ingredients combine into such a pleasant drink. Dried apricots have a great nutrient profile and add a beautiful caramel-type sweetness. Delicious!

First blend

8 brazil nuts in 1 cup water (or use nut milk or plain water)

Then add

4 apricots (dried) chopped
1 banana (frozen or fresh)
1 cup berries (frozen)
2 cups greens (mild/mild or mild/strong)

Ice

Recommendation

Best to use organic unsulfured dried apricots (they are dark in color)

40. On Blueberry Dill

Light and refreshing and a winner in the points department

> 1 cup water
> 1 cup blueberries (frozen)
> 1 apple (without the stalk, chopped)
> ¼ cup dill
> 1 celery stalk
> 1.5 cups mild greens

Ice

41. Raspberry Serenade

Herb-ing up your smoothie is another way to up your benefits and your green quota. The apple provides just the right amount of sweetness to balance the raspberries and cilantro.

> 1 cup water
> 1 cup raspberries (frozen)
> 1 apple (minus the stalk, chopped)
> ¼ cup cilantro/coriander
> 1 celery stalk
> 1.5 cup mild greens (go on, test this out with a small amount of strong greens too)

Ice

42.   Mango Carob Dessert Smoothie

This is based on my famous *Vanilla Pudding* smoothie series. It scores full marks for many drinkers!

Blend first

> 1 cup water
> ½ cup cashews (soaked if you have them available, dry will do)
> 3 dates (or other dried fruit)

Then add:

> 2 tbsp carob
> 1 small avocado, or half a large
> 1 cup mango (frozen or fresh)
> 2 cups mild greens
> ¼ - ½ tsp cinnamon
> Vanilla
> Pinch sea salt

Ice as desired

Recommendation

> Dried peaches or apricots taste wonderful in this smoothie. Soak them (adding soak water too) if you want them very smooth.

43.   Mango Crème Carabel

This is based on my famous *Vanilla Pudding* smoothie series. A flavor sensation in its own right. And besides, you need several variations so you can keep on enjoying this one.

Blend first

> 1 cup water
> ½ cup cashews (soaked if you have them available, dry will do)
> 3 dates (or dried apricots)

Then add:

> 1 cup mango (frozen or fresh)
> 1 small avocado, or half a large
> 2 cups mild greens
> ½ cup mint
> 2 tbsp carob
> ¼ - ½ tsp cinnamon
> Vanilla
> Pinch sea salt

Ice as desired

44. Minted Crème Carabel

Carob can be substituted by cacao or cacao nibs if you like. It's all good!

Blend first

    1 cup water
    ½ cup cashews (soaked if you have them available, dry will do)
    3 soft dates (or soaked dried fruit)

Then add:

    Up to 2 tbsp carob
    1 cup mint
    1 small avocado, or half a large
    1 cup mild greens
    ¼ - ½ tsp cinnamon optional
    Vanilla
    Pinch sea salt

1 cup ice

45.   Bananazilla Smoothie

The last one to round out the collection from my famous *Vanilla Pudding* smoothie series.

Blend first

  1 cup water
  ½ cup cashews or 8 brazil nuts (soaked if you have them available, dry will do)
  2 dates or dried figs

Then add:

  1 small avocado, or half a large
  1 banana (frozen or fresh)
  2 cups mild greens
  2 tbsp carob
  ¼ - ½ tsp cinnamon
  Vanilla
  Pinch sea salt

Ice as desired

46. Date With An Orange

Believe it or not, some folk just don't like oranges. Robert (my husband) is one of those. However he LOVES this scrumptious smoothie. Go figure.

    1 orange
    1 stalk celery
    2 cups mild greens (try romaine/cos or mizuna or your choice from the list)
    1 cup water
    2 dates (optional – I like to add the dates last in the blend to feel the sweet specks of fruit)

Add ½ cup ice (towards end of blending)

Recommendation

If you prefer to avoid dates, the result will be good with other dried fruit. For example add soaked dried peaches or apricots.

47. Orange Cinnamon Paradiso

Transform your Date with an Orange (above) into a cinnamon-lover's delight. It really is different enough to deserve its own page.

    1 orange
    2 dates, remove the pits
    1 stalk celery
    1 cup greens
    1 cup water
    ¼ tsp or more of cinnamon

½ cup ice (towards end of blending)

48. The B.O.S.S.

Another instant transformation. Basil complements the orange and gives complexity to this delicious smoothie. Surprisingly, my daughter loves this and gives it an 8!

1 orange
2 dates
1 stalk celery
1 cup greens
1 cup water
¼ cup basil (or more if you're game)

Add ½ cup ice (towards end of blending)

Recommendation

Substitute other dried fruit for dates. Soak them if you like.

49. Tomango Fandango

The title is clever enough. Do you really expect me to come up with some clever quip every single page? LOL Oh, OK, scoring a very good 7.5 from the kid-in-residence, it's surprisingly fresh and delicious.

1 cup mango (frozen)
2 tomatoes
1 cup water
½ cup basil
2 cups greens (any combination)
1-3 tsp lime juice (or lemon) to taste

Ice

50. Pacific Paradise

Yes, it's great. Just ask my family. Isabelle scores this one 9.75. Robert scores it 10. LOL

 2 kiwi
 2 apple
 2 cups greens
 ¼ tsp cinnamon
 ½-1 cup water
 Sea salt

Add ice

51. Summer Lite

Isabelle gives this a whopping 9.75. You'll see that I recommend an optional dash of cayenne pepper. Of course my daughter didn't want this final spicy variation, but it's also delicious.

 1 pear
 1 cup water
 3-4 dates (soft medjool are ideal, no pits)
 ½ cup coriander
 2 cups greens

Add ½ - 1 cup ice

Recommendation

 Optional: Try a pinch of cayenne pepper.
 Substitute different dried fruit for texture; figs,
 apricots, peaches, raisins. Soaked or un-soaked
 (blender and taste-dependent).

52.   Savory Spice

Yes, this decidedly savory smoothie does have a list of ingredients as long as your arm, but they are all easy to find. Oh, and it is packed with greens. If you don't like chilli peppers or cayenne, either reduce the amount or leave it out. The stronger greens (watercress, rocket, mustard leaves) do really well in this little number. Personal preferences will dictate your choices. The avocado makes it creamy.

¼ cup beet
½ cup red pepper (capsicum)
½ avocado
1 stalk celery, chopped
¼ cup broccoli
¼ cup parsley
¼ cup cilantro/coriander (optional extra)
2 cups greens (suggestion 1 cup mild and 1 cup strong greens)
1 tbsp onion chopped
1 small clove of garlic
1 small red chilli pepper or a pinch of cayenne

Add 1 cup of water and ice as desired

Recommendation

Another blended salad-type savory smoothie: Popular, I like it, but it's not a universal favorite. Hey, you can count on me to tell you the truth!

53.   Berry Cress

EVERYONE likes this – even with the cress! If you get a chance soak your sunflower seeds anywhere up to 2 hours to activate them (which softens them for the blend). You may like to blend them with a cup of water first before adding the other ingredients if your blender needs help.

¼ sunflower seeds (preferably soaked)
1 cup water
2 cups watercress (or rocket, or any green of your choice)
½ cup blueberries (frozen or fresh)
1 cup raspberries
3-4 dates or other soft dried fruit

Add ice and more water if needed

54. Kiwi Krave

Everyone liked this one. It's satisfyingly good!

2 kiwi
1 mango (flesh only of course!) frozen
½ cup coriander
1.5 cups mild greens
1 cup water

Ice

Recommendation

Optional: Add ¼ cup parsley

55. Beet This!

This one is REALLY great with a cup or 2 of watercress or other strong green in any proportion you choose. It's hard to beet! (hehehe)

1 cup water
1 kiwi
2 cups greens (kale and or spinach or romaine lettuce, remember to try with some strong greens too)
½ cup beet chopped
1 cup blueberries
1 orange (no peel)
Optional: A little nub of ginger

Add ice

56.   Heavenly Rocket

It's got rocket in the title, but feel free to add in some sorrel for that lovely lemony flavor. Hmmm... 1 cup rocket and 1 cup sorrel ... heavenly.

Blend first

> 8 brazil nuts
> 1 cup water (or nut milk or if you prefer use water only)

Then add

> 2 cups rocket (or other strong green such as watercress)
> OR 1 cup mild greens + 1 cup rocket
> 1 cup mango (frozen or fresh)

Add ice and water according to your whim

Recommendation

> Use ¼ cup different nuts or seeds
> Put in a slurp of coconut oil

57.   Mint Skyrocket

The emphasis here is on the mango mint. You'll be surprised how well the flavor of a slightly spicier green like rocket or watercress blends with the mango!

1 coconut water or nut milk
1 cup mango
1 cup rocket
1 cup mint

Add more ice and water to desired thickness and temperature

58.   Green Rocket Booster

Similar to the one above but with extra greens and less of a mango flavor. Sometimes you just want to 'go green'. This one has a massive 3 cups of greens.

Blend first:

¼ cup cashews
1 cup water

Then add:

2 cups rocket or watercress (or 1 cup mild and 1 cup rocket)
1 cup mint
1 cup mango (fresh or frozen)

Add more ice and water to desired thickness and temperature.

Recommendation

Add another ½ cup of mango if you wish.

59.   Tropical Vertigo

With 3 cups of greens and 2 cups of tropical fruit it's a massively healthy combination.

Blend first:

2 tbsp sesame seeds
1 cup water

Then add:

1 cup pineapple
1 cup mango
1 cup rocket
1 cup mild greens
1 cup mint

Add more ice and water to desired thickness and temperature.

60. Raspberry Banana Sunshine

Superbly healthful sunflower seeds can have quite an impact on the taste of these blended drinks. They're best to use with the stronger tasting fruit. Raspberries and bananas do well here. Another favorite with the kids.

Blend first

¼ cup sunflower seeds
1 cup water

Then add

1.5 cups raspberries (frozen)
1 banana
2 cups greens (any combination of mild greens)

Add more ice and water to desired thickness and temperature.

61.   Pineapple Pick-Me-Up

An unquestionably refreshing, lemony, summer smoothie

> 1 cup water
> 1 cup ripe (sweet) pineapple
> 1 tomato
> 1 tbsp lime
> ¼ cup broccoli
> ¼ cup cilantro
> 1 cup rocket
> 1 cup mild greens (try cabbage or mizuna)
> Pinch of sea salt

Ice

62.   Chocolate Charm

What? Cabbage in a smoothie? Boy, are you in for a surprise. What a way to enhance your nutrition by using yet another green in your smoothies. As usual I am recommending cacao nibs instead of cacao. While cocoa is less bitter, if you want to use cacao, take it easier on the powder by adding small amounts at a time to get your desired result. Carob also gives a great result!

First blend

> ¼ cup almonds
> 1 cup of water (almond milk or other nut milk)

Then add the following

> 1 banana (frozen or fresh)
> 1 cup mild greens
> 1 cup cabbage
> 1 tsp vanilla or more to taste (I like strong vanilla in this one and place 2 tsp)
> Up to ¼ tsp sea salt
> ¼ cup cacao nibs (or if you don't have cacao nibs then add cacao powder to taste, 1 tsp at a time).

Ice and water as desired

63. Strawberry Mint Memento

1 cup strawberries (fresh or frozen, hulled)
1 avocado
1 cup water
1 cup cabbage
1 cup mild greens (try sweet potato leaves, asparagus lettuce, bok choy, or spinach)
½ to 1 cup mint
2 dates to sweeten

Ice and water to reach desired temperature and consistency

Recommendation

Other sweeteners include dried figs, dried peaches or dried apricots (stevia or agave syrup).

64. Carob-Mint Caress

1 cup strawberries (frozen or fresh)
2 tbsp carob powder
1 avocado
1 cup cabbage
1 cup mild greens (sweet potato leaves, asparagus lettuce, bok choy, baby spinach)
½ cup mint
2 dates
1 cup water

Ice as desired

Recommendation

Try this with ¼ cup raw cacao nibs instead of the carob powder
Other sweeteners to try are dried figs, dried peaches or dried apricots instead of dates (stevia or agave syrup).

65. Red Rocket Smoothie

Loads of green yet as spicy red as you wish! This one's definitely savory. Great with lots of ice on a hot summer's day.

> 1 cup water
> ½ cup red capsicum
> ½ cup broccoli
> ½ cup cucumber
> 1 small chilli (strength can be unpredictable so start with ½) you could use a pinch of cayenne pepper
> 1 small clove garlic
> 1 tbsp onion
> 1 cup rocket

Ice and water to desired temperature and consistency

Recommendation

> You could try this one without the onion and garlic
> Add basil, some sea salt and cracked pepper

66. Tropical Red Rocket

I like the sweet and savory nature of this one. The mango and pineapple give it that tropical feel. As with anything if you have a preference you can change the proportions or eliminate the onion and garlic. I like the variety (and the nutrition) that this recipe brings.

1 cup water
½ cup mango
½ cup pineapple
½ cup red capsicum
½ cucumber
½ cup broccoli
1 cup rocket
1 small chilli (if unsure start with half)
1 small clove garlic
1 tbsp onion

Add ice and water to your desired temperature and consistency

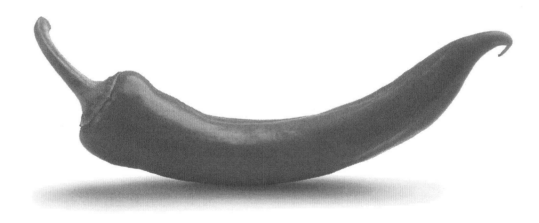

67.   CeleryBration

Sounds kinda plain, tastes really great. This one scored 9! Robert prefers to leave out the onion.

    1 celery stalk
    ½ cup broccoli
    ½ cup basil
    ½ avocado
    2 cups greens (1 mild and 1 strong, or any favored combination. Try spinach along with rocket/watercress)
    1 cup water
    1 tbsp onion (optional if you don't like the 'bite')
    1 tbsp lime or lemon juice
    Pinch salt

Blend in ice as desired

68.   Pineapple Earth-Shaker

I love this adaptable potion because you can play around with it depending on how spicy you love your food and really appreciate the differences. Vary the proportion of strong greens you want to use. You may like to start with 2 cups of mild greens and work your way up on the spice 'Richter Scale'. Two cups of mustard leaves is not for the feint hearted!

In fact the mustard leaves seem to get spicier the longer I leave this smoothie. On the other hand, 2 cups of watercress is very doable for most people. With the mild leaves I can promise you that this one is another winner from the resident 9 year old (scoring 8).

    2 cups greens (mild/mild, mild/strong or strong/strong)
    1 cup pineapple (frozen or fresh)
    1 stalk celery
    ½ cup basil
    1 tomato
    ½ avocado
    1 cup water

Ice for temperature, consistency and taste

69. Pineapple Pesto

A top scorer! There's something eminently delicious about balancing sweetness with a strong herb like basil.

1 cup pineapple
1 celery stalk
½ cup basil
½ cup broccoli
½ avocado
2 cups greens (mild/mild or mild/strong)
1 tbsp onion (optional)
1 tbsp lime or lemon juice
1 cup water

Ice

70. Aromango

You can make this one with either mild or strong greens. Its sweet and savory nature lends itself to both. I am very partial to rocket and watercress for this because of the balance with the basil, lime and mango! The avocado softens the mouth feel.

1 cup mango
½ avocado
½ cup broccoli
½ cup basil
1 celery stalk
1 cup mild or strong greens (try spinach or try rocket/watercress)
1 tbsp onion
1 tbsp lime or lemon juice

Use 1 cup water and some ice to achieve your desired temperature and consistency.

71.   Bright Limey

Bright and fresh with a little sweet and sour going on. Another highly scoring (8-9) smoothie from everyone including my mom, hubby and 9 year old girl.

2 apples (no stalk, chopped)
1 cup water
2 cups kale (or other mild greens)
2 tbsp lemon or lime juice

Blend in some ice to reach the desired temperature and consistency!

72. Classic Pear Smoothie

One of the classics. It's great to rely on such a simple recipe.

1.5 - 2 pears (regular size, no stalk, chopped)
1 cup water
2 cups strong greens (or 1 cup mild and 1 cup strong)
2 tbsp lemon or lime juice

Ice as desired

Recommendation

Add cinnamon, vanilla and salt

73. Silky Pear

Texture is such an important part of the taste experience.

The avocado makes the classic pear smoothie even smoother and less citrusy.

1.5 - 2 pears (regular size, no stalk, chopped)
1 cup water
½ avocado (or 1 small)
2 cups strong greens (or 1 cup mild and 1 cup strong)
2 tbsp lemon or lime juice

Ice as desired

Recommendation

Add cinnamon, vanilla and salt

74. Mon Pear

1.5 - 2 pears (regular size, no stalk, chopped)
½ avocado (or 1 small)
1 cup water
1 cup mint
1 cup mild or strong greens (try sorrel)
2 tbsp lemon or lime juice

Ice as desired

75. The Green Smile

Mmmmm... use mild greens here to let the lime and basil really stand out!

2 apples (no stalk, chopped)
½ avocado
1 cup water
½ cup basil
½ cup broccoli
2 cups mild greens (try kale, cabbage, spinach, tatsoi, mizuna)
2 tbsp lemon or lime juice

Add ice and water as desired

76. Pine Zinger

1 cup water
1 cup mango (frozen or fresh)
1 cup pineapple
1 small piece of ginger
½ cup broccoli
1.5 cups of mild greens (try romaine/cos, spinach, chickweed)

Ice

77. Strawbanana Crush

While not very sweet this smoothie is sure to refresh you. My daughter gets rather specific with her scoring. She gave this 8.75. You gotta love it.

1 cup water
1.5 cups strawberries (frozen or fresh)
1 banana
2 cups mild leaves (spinach, kale, chickweed)
2 dates
¼ - ½ cup cilantro/coriander

Add water or ice to create the desired temperature and consistency. Remember if you're using fresh strawberries you will probably need at least a cup of ice.

78. Salsa Me Smooth

So packed full of greens, so tasty.

1 cup water
¼ cup beetroot
1 cup pineapple (OR 1 apple)
½ cup red bell pepper/capsicum
¼ cup broccoli
¼ - ½ cup coriander
1 stalk celery
2 cups mild greens (try butter lettuce or wandering jew, purslane ...)
2-4 tsp of lemon juice (to taste, start with 2 tsp)
Small piece of ginger
Optional pinch of cayenne pepper

Ice and water as desired

79. Quick And Easy Mint Smoothie

Just what the title says, quick and easy. This does need a little sweetening agent. I always prefer to put dried fruit in such as dried figs, dried apricots, peaches, rather than opting for agave or stevia. The other way to sweeten it could be with half a nice ripe pear.

1 cup water
1 cup mint
1 cup mild greens
½ avocado
2 dried fruit (see sweetening ideas above) or soft dates

Add ice and blend for your desired temperature and consistency

80. Quick And Easy Mint Smoothie Mark 2

This is very simple to make and there's not much to it. You can't ignore the 9.9 near perfect scoring from the resident kid on hand.

Blend ¼ cup cashews with 1 cup water

Then add

1 cup mint
1 cup mild greens
2 cup ice
2 dried fruit or soft dates

81. Berry Appealing

I like this one because of its hint of natural sweetness. Feel free to add a date or other sweetener if needed. Family and friends liked it the way it is. You'll find that the sea salt actually brings out the sweetness of the berries!

1 cup water
1.5 cups frozen mixed berries (your choice or from a prepack)
½ avocado
¼ cup parsley
1 cup mild greens (try mizuna, spinach, kale)
1 cup strong green (try rocket)
2 pinches sea salt (up to ¼ tsp)
Pinch cayenne pepper

Add ice as desired and blend

Recommendation

Optional: Add a couple of soft (medjool or other) dates without the stones! Or dried fruit or agave syrup if you desire.

82.   Classic Banana

This is a simple basic formula. It's included because it works. I don't know about you, but sometimes you need to be reminded how simple it can be and how wonderful it is to return to the basics!

2 bananas (frozen or fresh)
2 cups of baby spinach or other mild greens
1 cup water

Add ice to create desired temperature and consistency

Recommendation

Variation: Add ¼ tsp cinnamon

83. Classic Mango

Get back to basics with this very simple smoothie. Works every time.

2 cups mango frozen or flesh of 2 mangos
2 cups of baby spinach or other mild greens
1 cup water

Add ice to create desired temperature and consistency

Recommendation

Variation: Add ¼ tsp cinnamon
Spices and ginger also complement this recipe

84. Coco-De-Menthe

1 cup coconut water
1 cup pineapple
½ avocado (or flesh of a young coconut)
½ - 1 cup mint leaves
2 cups spinach leaves (or any combination of mild greens)
Pinch salt

Recommendation

Vanilla and cinnamon optional
Nut milk (with cashews) works very well

85.   Classic Strawberry

Strawberries are sometimes not very sweet so unless your berries are of the sweeter kind you will have to add something. I have suggested dried figs. They are sweet and caramel-like and also have seeds which complement the seeds in the strawberries. Or add any dried fruit, an apple, or soft dates (less recommended are agave, honey or stevia). For a smoother blend than figs, add dates or dried peaches.

1 cup water
2 cup strawberries (frozen or fresh)
½ avocado
2 dried figs, chopped (remove the hard stalk)
2 cups of greens (I use 1 cup mild and 1 cup strong such as watercress)
Lime juice to taste

Water and or ice as required

86.   Rocket Mango Tango

You'll always win me over with mango. This one is basic, reliable and one of my favorites. Check the strength of your rocket before you commit. The rocket and mango are just great together.

2 cups rocket (or substitute partly or fully with mild greens)
1.5 cups mango (fresh or frozen)
1 cup water

Ice and water as you need them

87.   Gone Troppo

This smoothie also highlights the delight of a strong green balanced by sweet fruit. Check out the variations suggested. You can get creative with herbs and spices.

2 cups rocket (or substitute partly or fully with mild greens)
½ cup mango
½ cup pineapple
1 cup water

Ice

Recommendations

Variations:

Add cinnamon
Add ½ cup cilantro
Add cayenne pepper
Add a little cumin (surprising!)

88.   Majestic Mango Mint

This combination is one of my personal favorites.

1 cup mango (fresh or frozen)
1.5 cup watercress
½- 1 cup mint
1 cup water

Add ice as desired and blend

89.   Velvet Mango Mint

1 cup mango
½ avocado
2 cups watercress
(or partly substitute with mild greens)
½ - 1 cup mint
1 cup water

Ice as required

90.   Apple Tang

A refreshing blend of lime, basil and apple. I always like to start by adding half the amount of lime and lemon to any recipe. It helps me control the outcome. It's easy to add.

2 apples
1 cup broccoli
1 cup water
1 cup mild greens
2 tbsp lime juice (use lemon if you don't have lime)
½ cup basil

Add ice as required and blend

91. Coco-Nana

When you add dried figs to your smoothie it adds a golden natural sweetness. The seeds add a little texture. The cilantro lifts the flavors beautifully.

    1 cup coconut water (plain water works too)
    2 dried figs chopped
    1 banana
    2 cups mild greens (try cabbage, spinach, sweet potato leaves)
    ½ cup coriander

Ice as required and blend

92. Kiwi Parsley Punch

Packs a parsley punch without a strong taste of parsley.

Blend first:

¼ cup cashews
2 medjool or other soft date (remove stones)
1 cup water

Then add

2 kiwi (remove the hard stalky end but keep the skin)
2 cups mild greens (try cabbage, spinach, chickweed)
½ cup parsley

Ice as desired and blend

Recommendation

Can use other dried fruit instead of fig.

93. Italian Summer

Picture sunning yourself on a restaurant balcony overlooking the Amalfi Coast, tasting the undeniably Mediterranean taste of basil perfectly balanced with tomato, greens and fruit. Aaaaaaaah :)

To 1 cup water add:

1 apple
½ cup guava (I use frozen guava so I don't need to negotiate the seeds which can sometimes be like little stones)
1 tomato
½ cup basil
2 cups greens (try 1 cup spinach and 1 cup rocket or 2 cups mild)

Ice as desired.

94.   Not Just Peachy

Fresh peaches are just divine. But if they aren't in season, try using 2 dried peach halves. You'll have the wonderful mouth feel and the burst of peachy sweetness that complements the cilantro and mango.

  1 peach
  1 cup mango
  2 cups mild greens
  ½ cup coriander/cilantro
  Optional; lemon juice to taste (start with 1 tsp)

Recommendations

  Try substituting strong greens for either part or all of the 2 cups of mild ones. You could experiment with watercress, rocket or endive.
  If you like lemon then use 2 cups of sorrel as your greens component (add the lemon juice later). Delicious.

95.   Cinnamon Celery Sensation

This light and mild smoothie has a good cinnamon flavor. It's not very sweet.

  1 banana
  1 stalk celery
  ½ cup parsley
  2 cups mild greens
  ½ tsp cinnamon
  1 cup water

Ice and water for desired temperature and consistency

96.   English Pears

Put on your airs and drink these pears. Oh so delicious. Perfect combination with cucumber sandwiches. Actually no, but I couldn't resist the reference to another British 'gourmet' standard. Pinky fingers up at the ready!

1 pear (no stalk, but keep the rest)
1 banana
2 cups greens
1 big handful of mint
1 cup water

Ice as required

97. Cream Apple-Mint

There's just about no better complement to apple than mint. This smoothie is definitely green with sour and sweet notes made creamy with the avocado. (While you're at it, check out the recommended variation too.) You know, if you don't have coconut water you can just add water. It doesn't change the flavor profile dramatically. It is on all counts decidedly refreshing.

> 1 cup coconut water
> ½ avocado
> 2 apples
> 2 soft dates (medjool, honey dates or other)
> 1 big handful of mint
> 1.5 cups of mild greens

Ice as desired.

Recommendation

> Pssst ... if you want to use something different to an avocado for creaminess and fresh young coconuts are available then scoop out the flesh and add it instead.

98. Loves Me Like A Brocc

> 1 large orange (peeled of course and chopped. Remove seeds if you like)
> ½ avocado
> 1 cup broccoli florets
> 1 cup mild greens (try spinach, romaine, lambsquarters)
> 1 cup water
> ½ tsp cinnamon
> 2 dried figs chopped (remove hard stalk)

Add ice to final blend

99. Perfectly Peared

... and highly scored. 9/10 from the folks I gave this one to. The watercress really balances the sweet of the pear and the complexity of the orange.

1 avocado
2 cups watercress
1 pear
1 orange
1 cup water

Ice as desired

100. StrawPear-Ease

I know this has one more ingredient than *Perfectly Peared*, but believe me when I say that adding strawberries transforms it into a unique smoothie. I guess you know by now that you can substitute mild greens in if you are not partial to the entire amount being stronger.

1 avocado
2 cups watercress
1 pear
1 orange
½ cup strawberries (fresh or frozen)
1 cup water

Ice as desired

101. Tropical Surprise

I don't know if I have said this but my hubby actually doesn't eat fruit much. Well he does eat the fruit that we count as vegetables (tomatoes, avocados, cucumbers, red bell peppers and so on) but when it comes to mangos and pineapples, well he would rather leave them be.

By the way he can't stand bananas. So imagine my surprise when he gave this invention the lofty score of 9.5 out of 10.

> 2 cups mustard leaves (or watercress, endive or rocket)
> 1 cup mango
> 1 banana
> 1 cup pineapple
> 1 cup water

Ice as desired

Recommendation

With mustard leaves this one could be very spicy so taste test them first.

102. Herbed Cleanser

I love the taste of dill. It refreshes and cleanses the palate all at the same time leaving you feeling light and free. This concoction is just lovely!

> 1 avocado
> 1 cup water
> 2 apples
> ¼ cup broccoli
> ½ dill
> 1.5 cup watercress or other strong green (substitute partly or wholly with mild greens)
> 1-2 tbsp lemon juice
> A little ginger

Ice as desired

103. Sweet Sunrise

This is a high ranking smoothie for sure. I love adding a small amount of sunflower seeds to a smoothie. Too much and it's overwhelming so I have found that ¼ cup does the trick. Blend with water first (if your blender is not so powerful otherwise throw everything in at one time). Sunflower seeds have high amounts of iron and vitamin B12 and so are wonderfully nutritious.

Blend first

> ¼ cup sunflower seeds
> Water

Then add and blend

> 1 peach or 2 dried peach halves
> 1 orange
> 2 dates (optional, or use dried fruit)
> 1 cup cabbage and 1 cup chickweed OR 2 cups mild greens
> A little ginger

Ice as desired

104. Dappled Greens

I love the way smoothies find a way to get ingredients together you may not have considered as partners before. The banana and dill work well and that was much to my surprise.

> 2 apples
> 1 banana (frozen or fresh)
> 2 dates or dried figs
> ¼ - ½ cup dill
> 2 cups mild greens (try cabbage, spinach or chickweed)
> 1 cup water

Ice as desired

105. Strawberry Dills Forever

1 apple (medium to large)
1 banana (frozen)
1 cup strawberries
¼ - ½ cup dill
2 dates or dried figs
2 cups mild greens (try cabbage and spinach, or chickweed)
1 cup water

Ice as required

106. Minted Blue

½ cup blueberries (fresh or frozen)
1 orange, peeled (no pips)
1 cup strawberries (fresh or frozen)
1 cup mint
1 cup mild greens
1 cup water

Ice as desired

Recommendations

Variation

Can substitute parsley for mint
What the heck, add parsley and mint!

107. Raspberry Crush

This smoothie has a lot of texture. Lots of seeds to give it a little mouth feel rather than having it completely smooth. You'll find the difference quite invigorating. Regardless of your blender quality I still recommend blending the sesame seeds first to get them ground down more finely.

First blend

¼ cup sesame seeds
1 cup water

Then add

1.5 cups raspberries (frozen)
½ avocado
2 dried figs (chopped)
¼ cup coconut (shredded)
1 tbsp flaxseeds
2 cups mild greens (your choice)
Either ¼ cup cacao nibs (my preference) OR add cacao powder to taste

Ice as desired

Recommendation

You could use 2 tablespoons of carob powder to replace the cacao.
Add in some chia seeds or chia gel.

108. Pear-ly There

Don't be deceived! This green smoothie with barely any ingredients packs a flavor punch that is very delightful. My hubby scored this one 10/10 and he doesn't even like oranges.

1 pear
1 orange
2 cups watercress (substitute partly or wholly with mild greens if you must)
½ cup broccoli florets
1 cup water

Add ice and blend

109. Basil Beauty

Although this is based on the *Pear-ly There* recipe, the addition of this fragrant herb completely changes its profile. Again, a wonderful combination. This one also scored a 10/10 from my sweet-fruit phobic husband!

1 pear
1 orange
½ cup broccoli florets
2 cups watercress
½ cup basil
1 cup water

Add ice and blend

Recommendation

Add avocado if you want something a little thicker.

110. Raspberry Dream

Blend first:

    1 cup water
    Handful of walnuts or pecans (or use nut or coconut milk)

Then add

    ½ avocado
    1 kiwi
    1 apple
    1 cup raspberries (frozen or fresh)
    2 cups mild greens
    1 cup water

Ice

Recommendation

Definitely try this with 2 cups watercress instead of mild greens. It should have its own title it's that good!

111. Bali Sunrise

My staple breakfast on Bali holidays (pre-GS days) was pineapple and papaya blended together (and a dash of lime).

    1 cup pineapple
    1 cup papaya (paw paw)
    2 cups mild greens
    ½ cup cilantro/coriander
    1 cup water

Add ice as required.

Recommendation

Try using ½ cup mint instead of the cilantro.
Try a dash of lime in any variant of this smoothie.

112. Minty Miracle

This is a truly great and very green (in fact lime green) smoothie. It's a family favorite.

   1 orange
   1 kiwi
   2 dates
   2 cups mild greens
   ½ cup mint
   1 cup water

Ice as required

Recommendation

Try using ½ cup coriander instead of mint.
Substitute dried peaches for dates.

113. Dessert Pear

A sweet tasty smoothie which regularly scores 9 out of 10.

1 pear
1 cup strawberries (frozen or fresh)
1 kiwi
1 cup water
2 cups mild greens (or include 1 cup watercress and 1 cup mild)
A good squeeze of lemon

Ice as required

114.   Refreshingly Herbal Pear

If you like a refreshing lightly herbed smoothie with fruit (and don't we all?) then this one is very agreeable. Mildly different in ingredients but really quite different in flavor to *Dessert Pear*. It also scores 8-9.

½ cup cilantro
1 pear
1 kiwi
1 cup strawberries
2 cups mild greens
1 cup water

Ice as required

115.   Sweet Dill Surprise

1 cup pineapple
¼ cup dill
1 banana (frozen)
2 cups greens (I am partial to 1 cup watercress and 1 cup mild)
1 cup water

Ice

116. Savory Papaya

1 cup papaya (pawpaw)
1 cup fennel
2 cups greens (both mild or 1 mild and 1 rocket or watercress)
1 or 2 pinches sea salt
1 cup water

Ice

117. Sweet Savory Papaya

1 cup papaya
1 cup pineapple
1 cup fennel
2 cups greens (mild/mild or mild/strong)
Pinch salt
1 cup water

Ice as required

118. Pakito Kicker

Feeling brave or need a kick, then substitute some strong greens for the mild ones, anywhere from ½ to 1.5 cups for those who really want to test those taste buds.

    1 cup papaya
    1 kiwi
    1 tomato
    ½ cup cilantro
    1.5 cups mild greens
    1 cup water

Ice as required

119. Pakito Kiss

Smooth, fruity, surprisingly good.

    1 cup papaya
    ½ cup pineapple
    1 kiwi
    1 tomato
    ½ avocado
    ½ cup cilantro
    1.5 cups mild greens (or substitute according to your mood with strong greens)

Add ice to your taste!

120. Amazing Grape

This smoothie is very adaptable. You can add herbs and even other fruit.

    1 cup grapes (seedless)
    1 pear (no stalk)
    ½ avocado
    2 cups mild greens
    1 cup water

Add ice as required

Recommendation

Variations:

    Add mint (exchange some mild greens)
    Use some non-dairy yogurt
    Add a frozen banana

121. Lemon Spinner

A really pleasant lemon sensation. The next 2 smoothies build on this basic recipe to provide ever more interesting results.

    ½ cup cucumber
    2 tbsp or more lemon juice
    1 tomato
    2 cups mild greens
    1 avocado
    1 cup water

Ice as required

122. Lemony Sippet

Greens-boosted for your drinking pleasure!

½ cup cucumber
2 tbsp or more lemon juice
1 tomato
2 cups mild greens
½ cup parsley
1 avocado
1 cup water

Ice

123. Lemon Digestive

Add the digestive power of the enzyme papain in the papaya and feel the difference.

½ cup cucumber
2 tbsp or more lemon juice
1 tomato
1 cup papaya (pawpaw)
2 cups mild greens
1 avocado
1 cup water

Ice

Recommendation

Add ½ cup of pineapple for a little more sweetness. Not too much because you already have a good amount of lemon juice in there!

124. Queen Of Cress

The more I use watercress in certain smoothies the more I like it. Maybe you will develop the taste for it too. It's flavorsome without being too strong (IMHO). You could make a 'greens exchange' for up to the entire 2 cups of watercress with mild greens. Here's what's in it ...

½ cup pineapple
1 kiwi
1 tomato
½ avocado
2 cups watercress (or substitute any greens of your choice)
½ cup mint or more
1 cup water

Ice

125. Papaya Cream Pudding

Use raw organic oatmeal if you can for this interesting blend. The oatmeal is soaked for a little while to soften it and plump it a tad. The papaya is stacked full of papain for great digestive benefit plus this mild fruit also adds to the creamy pudding texture.

I like this mild-mannered smoothie 2 ways. Either with a strong vanilla flavor (with or without adding more spices) ... or ... I add some lemon juice to it.

> ¼ cup oatmeal soaked in ¼ cup water
> 1 cup papaya
> 1 kiwi
> ½ avocado
> Sea salt (up to ¼ tsp)
> 1-2 tsp vanilla
> 1 cup coconut water

Ice as needed

Recommendation

> Add more vanilla and or lots of other spices (cinnamon, nutmeg, cloves or cardamom)
> Or add a good squeeze or 2 of lemon
> Add a tablespoon of coconut oil

126. Oatmeal Breakfast Smoothie

Packed with energy to sustain you through the morning this smoothie can be enjoyed sipped from a glass, or spooned from a bowl.

Oatmeal ¼ cup soaked in ¼ cup water
2 pieces of dried fruit
1-2 tsp vanilla
2 tbsp almonds
2 tbsp raisins
2 cups mild greens
½ avocado
Spices, try ¼ tsp cinnamon, nutmeg and a touch of cardamom

When smooth, top with a handful of raisins and some chopped nuts of your choice (almonds, brazil nuts, walnuts) or some sunflower seeds, pepitas. And then stir them through to complete your breakfast smoothie.

Recommendations

Great to try with carob or cacao powder.
Transform it into a raspberry oatmeal with a ½ cup of raspberries.
Swirl some honey or maple syrup over the top if that sounds good!

127. Ki-Wheat Wonder

Wheatgrass has a strong yet sweet taste. If you are not used to wheatgrass then I recommend starting with a small amount and work your way up. This green smoothie gets a little kick from the wheatgrass and is beautifully tangy.

2 kiwi
1 stalk celery
1.5 cups mild greens
¼ - ½ cup wheatgrass
1 cup water

Add ice as required

Recommendation

If you don't have wheatgrass growing at home then harvest a store-bought tray, add water, blend and then freeze in ice cube trays. I add 1-2 cubes (of course the number is going to depend on the size of your cubes!).

128. Ki-Wheat Minty Marvel

This is a variation on the Ki-Wheat Wonder. When you add mint it transforms it completely and makes it less tangy too.

2 kiwi
¼ - ½ cup wheatgrass (or 1-2 cubes of frozen wheatgrass)
1 stalk celery
1 cup mild greens
½ - 1 cup mint
1 cup water

Add ice to your taste!

Recommendation

You can batch blend a whole tray of wheatgrass with some water to freeze and store as ice cubes.

129. BlueGrass

The parsley is wonderful for neutralizing any excess tanginess of the wheatgrass.

1 cup blueberries (fresh or frozen)
1 apple
½ cup parsley
¼ - ½ cup wheatgrass (or 1-2 cubes frozen wheatgrass)
1 cup cabbage or other mild green
1 cup water

Add ice

Recommendation

If you find you have overdone the wheatgrass add some more parsley (and perhaps a bit more fruit).

130. Creamy Green Supreme

Smooth, sweet and satisfying.

½ avocado
1 pear
1 cup pineapple
¼ – ½ cup wheatgrass (or 1-2 frozen cubes)
1.5 cups mild greens
1 cup water

Add ice

Recommendation

Exchange 1 cup of your greens with 1 cup of mint. One of Robert's favorites. Wonderful!

131. Summer Meadows

1 orange
1 apple
1 cup strawberries (fresh or frozen)
¼ - ½ cup wheatgrass (or 1-2 frozen cubes)
½ cup parsley
1 cup mild greens
1 cup water

Add ice

132. Citrus Cocktail

Tangy citrus is just great to refresh and revitalize. Some people love grapefruit. If it's too bitter for you then either start with a segment or 2 and work up. Or feel free to leave it out because the smoothie will work well with just oranges and mandarins.

2 oranges
2 mandarins
½ - 1 grapefruit (optional)
½ cup parsley
2 cups mild greens
1 cup water

Add ice

Recommendation

Add ½ cup mint or exchange it for the parsley.

Thank You!

Thank you for reading this far – I hope that along the way you have taken the time to make a smoothie or two LOL!

I loved doing all the research and experimentation that led up to finalizing the 132 recipes and all their variations – and it proved to me that there are many, many ways to make a delicious smoothie.

I encourage you to do the same – experiment with your favorite smoothies from this book and continue your journey!

As always, I love hearing from you, whatever questions you have or feedback you may wish to share ... and if you've enjoyed and used this book, **please leave a review for me on Amazon** (you can use this easy link, it will redirect you to the review page: http://www.hotyogadoctor.com/gsm-review)– it will help me continue to improve this book and produce many others!

Here's a big green smoothie cheer to your vibrant health!

Gabrielle

info@hotyogadoctor.com

Recipe Index Cross-Referenced For Major Ingredient

You've arrived at the back of the book where I have put together a handy cross-referenced list of recipes grouped by major ingredient. If you didn't mean to come here, just click the link below to return to the Table of Contents!

(Click here to return to the main Table of Contents)

And now that you are here, let me tell you how to use this particular section (and I'll repeat a small portion from the section "***Recipe Index Cross-Referenced For Major Ingredient***".

In the following section you'll find ALL the recipes 1-132 in no particular order. I pondered this and discussed it endlessly - "should we 'categorize' the recipes etc?" - in the end we decided that the best method is to be constantly inspired and surprised by reading through and not to fall into choosing something you "think" you will like just because it falls into a "category".

But this can make it harder to see your chosen ingredient in a list of recipes ... so ... we made a "*Recipe Index*" which cross-references lists of recipes by major ingredient - think of it as a sub-table of contents.

So as not to complicate the book for new readers AND to keep the information and main Table of Contents clear, these are located here at the back of the book.

Apple/Pear

Avocado

Mango/Papaya

Banana

Pineapple

Berries

Citrus (Orange, Lemon, Lime)

Dried Fruit and Dates

Unconventional Smoothie Vegetables! (Beet/Carrot/Cucumber/Fennel/Garlic/Onion/Red Bell Pepper)

Nuts, Seeds or Nut/Seed Milk

Apple/Pear

5. Mango Delight 92

19. What A Lovely Pear 104

24. Blue Eyes Smoothie 108

32. Stevie's Punch 115

35. Minted Pear Smoothie 116

36. Lime Ginger Dill Smoothie 117

38. Fennel Refresher 119

40. On Blueberry Dill 121

41. Raspberry Serenade 121

50. Pacific Paradise 128

51. Summer Lite 128

71. Bright Limey 142

72. Classic Pear Smoothie 143

73. Silky Pear 143

74. Mon Pear 144

75. The Green Smile 144

90. Apple Tang 153

93. Italian Summer 155

96. English Pears 157

97. Cream Apple-Mint 158

99. Perfectly Peared 159

100. StrawPear-Ease 159

102. Herbed Cleanser 160

104. Dappled Greens 161

105. Strawberry Dills Forever 162

108. Pear-ly There 165

109. Basil Beauty 165

110. Raspberry Dream 166

113. Dessert Pear 168

114. Refreshingly Herbal Pear 169

120. Amazing Grape 172

129. BlueGrass 179

130. Creamy Green Supreme 179

131. Summer Meadows 180

Avocado

1. Classic Pine-Mint Smoothie 90

6. Vanilla Chai Smoothie 93

7. Choc-Chai Smoothie 94

8. Banana-Choc-Chai Smoothie 95

14. Saladicious 100

15. Salad Sunset 101

20. Tangy Tex Mex 105

22. Mango Spice 106

23. Choc-Mango Spice...107

25. Vanilla Pudding Smoothie...109

26. Carob Vanilla Spice Pudding Smoothie..110

27. Mint Vanilla Pudding Smoothie..111

31. Mint Magic...114

42. Mango Carob Dessert Smoothie...122

43. Mango Crème Carabel..123

44. Minted Crème Carabel...124

45. Bananazilla Smoothie...125

52. Savory Spice...129

63. Strawberry Mint Memento..136

64. Carob-Mint Caress..137

67. CeleryBration...140

68. Pineapple Earth-Shaker..140

69. Pineapple Pesto...141

70. Aromango...141

73. Silky Pear..143

74. Mon Pear..144

75. The Green Smile..144

79. Quick And Easy Mint Smoothie...147

81. Berry Appealing...148

84. Coco-De-Menthe...150

85. Classic Strawberry..151

89. Velvet Mango Mint 153

97. Cream Apple-Mint 158

98. Loves Me Like A Brocc 158

99. Perfectly Peared 159

100. StrawPear-Ease 159

102. Herbed Cleanser 160

119. Pakito Kiss 171

120. Amazing Grape 172

121. Lemon Spinner 172

122. Lemony Sippet 173

123. Lemon Digestive 174

124. Queen Of Cress 175

125. Papaya Cream Pudding 176

126. Oatmeal Breakfast Smoothie 177

130. Creamy Green Supreme 179

Mango/Papaya

2. Cinnamango Smoothie 91

3. Mangolicious Strawberry-Mint 91

5. Mango Delight 92

22. Mango Spice 106

23. Choc-Mango Spice 107

37. Poppy Celebration Smoothie 118

42. Mango Carob Dessert Smoothie 122

43. Mango Crème Carabel 123

49. Tomango Fandango 127

54. Kiwi Krave 130

56. Heavenly Rocket 131

57. Mint Skyrocket..132

58. Green Rocket Booster 132

59. Tropical Vertigo 133

66. Tropical Red Rocket 139

70. Aromango 141

76. Pine Zinger 144

83. Classic Mango 150

86. Rocket Mango Tango 151

87. Gone Troppo 152

88. Majestic Mango Mint 153

89. Velvet Mango Mint 153

94. Not Just Peachy 156

101. Tropical Surprise 160

111. Bali Sunrise 166

116. Savory Papaya 170

117. Sweet Savory Papaya 170

118. Pakito Kicker 171

119. Pakito Kiss 171

123. Lemon Digestive 174

125. Papaya Cream Pudding 176

Banana

4. Bananaberry Cream 92

8. Banana-Choc-Chai Smoothie 95

9. Banana Raspberry Yum 96

10. Berrylicious 97

18. Berry Packed Smoothie 103

30. Iron Maiden Smoothie 114

39. Apricana Smoothie 120

45. Bananazilla Smoothie 125

60. Raspberry Banana Sunshine 134

62. Chocolate Charm 135

77. Strawbanana Crush 145

82. Classic Banana 149

91. Coco-Nana 154

95. Cinnamon Celery Sensation 156

101. Tropical Surprise 160

104. Dappled Greens 161

105. Strawberry Dills Forever 162

115. Sweet Dill Surprise 169

Pineapple

1. Classic Pine-Mint Smoothie 90

11. Pineapple Broccoli Sensation 97

12. Pineapple Dilly Dally 98

15. Salad Sunset 101

17. Blueberry Pineapple Smoothie 103

19. What A Lovely Pear 104

20. Tangy Tex Mex 105

32. Stevie's Punch 115

37. Poppy Celebration Smoothie 118

59. Tropical Vertigo 133

61. Pineapple Pick-Me-Up 135

66. Tropical Red Rocket 139

68. Pineapple Earth-Shaker 140

69. Pineapple Pesto 141

76. Pine Zinger 144

78. Salsa Me Smooth 146

84. Coco-De-Menthe 150

87. Gone Troppo 152

101. Tropical Surprise 160

111. Bali Sunrise 166

115. Sweet Dill Surprise 169

117. Sweet Savory Papaya 170

119. Pakito Kiss 171

124. Queen Of Cress 175

130. Creamy Green Supreme 179

Berries

3. Mangolicious Strawberry-Mint 91

4. Bananaberry Cream 92

9. Banana Raspberry Yum 96

10. Berrylicious 97

16. Blue Bat 102

17. Blueberry Pineapple Smoothie 103

18. Berry Packed Smoothie 103

24. Blue Eyes Smoothie 108

30. Iron Maiden Smoothie 114

34. Strawberry Kiwi Sunshine 116

37. Poppy Celebration Smoothie 118

39. Apricana Smoothie 120

40. On Blueberry Dill 121

41. Raspberry Serenade 121

53. Berry Cress 129

55. Beet This! 130

60. Raspberry Banana Sunshine 134

77. Strawbanana Crush 145

81. Berry Appealing 148

100. StrawPear-Ease 159

106. Minted Blue 163

107. Raspberry Crush 164

110. Raspberry Dream 166

113. Dessert Pear 168

114. Refreshingly Herbal Pear 169

129. BlueGrass 179

Citrus (Orange, Lemon, Lime)

38. Fennel Refresher 119

46. Date With An Orange 126

47. Orange Cinnamon Paradiso 126

48. The B.O.S.S. 127

49. Tomango Fandango 127

55. Beet This! 130

61. Pineapple Pick-Me-Up 135

67. CeleryBration 140

69. Pineapple Pesto 141

70. Aromango 141

71. Bright Limey 142

72. Classic Pear Smoothie 143

73. Silky Pear 143

74. Mon Pear 144

75. The Green Smile 144

78. Salsa Me Smooth 146

85. Classic Strawberry 151

90. Apple Tang 153

98. Loves Me Like A Brocc 158

99. Perfectly Peared 159

100. StrawPear-Ease 159

102. Herbed Cleanser 160

103. Sweet Sunrise 161

106. Minted Blue 163

108. Pear-ly There 165

109. Basil Beauty 165

112. Minty Miracle 167

121. Lemon Spinner 172

122. Lemony Sippet 173

123. Lemon Digestive 174

131. Summer Meadows 180

132. Citrus Cocktail 180

Dried Fruit and Dates

6. Vanilla Chai Smoothie 93

7. Choc-Chai Smoothie 94

8. Banana-Choc-Chai Smoothie 95

25. Vanilla Pudding Smoothie 109

26. Carob Vanilla Spice Pudding Smoothie 110

27. Mint Vanilla Pudding Smoothie 111

28. Kiwi Vanilla Smoothie 112

29. Freshly Minted 113

31. Mint Magic 114

37. Poppy Celebration Smoothie 118

39. Apricana Smoothie 120

42. Mango Carob Dessert Smoothie 122

43. Mango Crème Carabel 123

44. Minted Crème Carabel 124

45. Bananazilla Smoothie 125

46. Date With An Orange 126

47. Orange Cinnamon Paradiso 126

48. The B.O.S.S. 127

51. Summer Lite 128

53. Berry Cress 129

63. Strawberry Mint Memento 136

64. Carob-Mint Caress 137

77. Strawbanana Crush 145

79. Quick And Easy Mint Smoothie 147

80. Quick And Easy Mint Smoothie Mark 2 147

85. Classic Strawberry 151

91. Coco-Nana 154

92. Kiwi Parsley Punch 155

94. Not Just Peachy 156

97. Cream Apple-Mint 158

98. Loves Me Like A Brocc 158

103. Sweet Sunrise 161

104. Dappled Greens 161

105. Strawberry Dills Forever 162

107. Raspberry Crush 164

112. Minty Miracle 167

126. Oatmeal Breakfast Smoothie 177

Unconventional Smoothie Vegetables!

(Beet/carrot/cucumber/fennel/garlic/onion/red bell pepper)

13. Herbal Ginger Beet 99

14. Saladicious 100

15. Salad Sunset 101

21. Dance To The Beet 105

36. Lime Ginger Dill Smoothie 117

38. Fennel Refresher 119

52. Savory Spice 129

55. Beet This! 130

65. Red Rocket Smoothie 138

66. Tropical Red Rocket 139

78. Salsa Me Smooth 146

116. Savory Papaya 170

117. Sweet Savory Papaya 170

121. Lemon Spinner 172

122. Lemony Sippet 173

123. Lemon Digestive 174

Nuts, Seeds or Nut/Seed Milk

3. Mangolicious Strawberry-Mint 91

6. Vanilla Chai Smoothie 93

7. Choc-Chai Smoothie 94

8. Banana-Choc-Chai Smoothie 95

18. Berry Packed Smoothie 103

22. Mango Spice 106

23. Choc-Mango Spice 107

25. Vanilla Pudding Smoothie 109

26. Carob Vanilla Spice Pudding Smoothie 110

27. Mint Vanilla Pudding Smoothie 111

28. Kiwi Vanilla Smoothie 112

29. Freshly Minted 113

32. Stevie's Punch 115

39. Apricana Smoothie 120

42. Mango Carob Dessert Smoothie 122

43. Mango Crème Carabel 123

44. Minted Crème Carabel 124

45. Bananazilla Smoothie 125

53. Berry Cress 129

56. Heavenly Rocket 131

58. Green Rocket Booster 132

59. Tropical Vertigo 133

60. Raspberry Banana Sunshine 134

62. Chocolate Charm 135

80. Quick And Easy Mint Smoothie Mark 2 147

92. Kiwi Parsley Punch 155

103. Sweet Sunrise 161

107. Raspberry Crush 164

110. Raspberry Dream 166

126. Oatmeal Breakfast Smoothie 177

Made in the USA
Middletown, DE
14 February 2015